Carbone's
COOKBOOK

Carbone's
COOKBOOK

JANE & MICHAEL STERN

With Recipes by Gaetano Carbone
and Vincent Carbone

RUTLEDGE HILL PRESS™

Nashville, Tennessee

A DIVISION OF THOMAS NELSON, INC.
www.ThomasNelson.com

To Charlie Carbone, Uncle Tony,
Frances Carbone, Billie Carbone,
and Angie Locario

Published by Rutledge Hill Press, a Division of Thomas Nelson, Inc., P.O. Box 141000, Nashville, Tennessee, 37214.

Photos on the title page and on pages xi, xii, xiii, xiv (bottom), 1, 2, 3, 4, 5, 23, 60, 78, 118, and 160 and on the color insert pages 1, 2 (inset), and 4 (bottom) are courtesy of Carbone's Restaurant.

Photos on pages xiv (top), 16, 22, 34, 52, 53, 69, 108, 140, 141, and 184 and on the color insert pages 2, 3, 4 (top), 5, 6, and 8 are by Michael Stern.

Library of Congress Cataloging-in-Publication Data

Stern, Jane.
    Carbone's cookbook / Jane & Michael Stern.
        p. cm.
    ISBN 1-4016-0122-7 (Hardcover)
    1. Cookery, Italian. 2. Cookery, American. 3. Carbone's (Restaurant) I. Stern, Michael, 1946– II. Title.
    TX723.S798 2003
    641.5945—dc22   2003015593

Printed in the United States of America

03 04 05 06 07—5 4 3 2 1

Contents

Foreword

Being the third generation and having the opportunity to carry on Carbone's reputation and traditions, I have the pleasure of telling you what a unique and wonderful experience this is. Although, admittedly, I do have some large shoes to fill.

I was first initiated into the realm of Carbone's as a small child. The restaurant was closed on Sundays, so after church my father, grandfather, and uncles would take the children to the restaurant to give our mothers a little break. The men folk would meet to talk business and to make us special snacks. My favorite was always the leftover sour dough bread turned into pizzas—something we call bruschetta. After a short business discussion, my grandfather would take us on an imaginary space ship ride from his control panel at the cappuccino machine. On these space voyages we would always find hidden treasures, usually loose change mysteriously placed under the dining booths. Hide and seek with my cousins was another favorite pastime at these gatherings.

As a teenager I was keenly aware that I was part of something special. My father, Guy, and his brother Carl were about to transform this neighborhood family restaurant into a fine-dining establishment. They wanted sophistication and comfort to blend with a customer service level that was on par with none. The customers were to be treated like our family. This was not an easy task, but determination abounds in our family and the dream became a reality.

I have met many wonderful people by being in this business. They include everyone from our valued patrons to our loyal staff. The best introduction I ever received, however, was the one to my wife, Olivia. There are so many stories to tell, and I am always amazed to hear new ones from customers who remember my grandfather Charlie, Uncle Tony, and Guy and Carl, who at the ages of 65 and 64 respectively are still known as "the boys" by our older patrons. I look forward to continuing the traditions as well as to improving the legacy of a true American Dream—Carbone's Restaurant.

Through the years the chefs of Carbone's have created a wonderful array of dishes still used today. Co-Executive Chef Paul Rafala pays tribute to the originators of these recipes:

One has to understand the statement that there is nothing new under the sun to begin to understand our strong convictions on the origin of these dishes. These dishes have been on and off the menus at Carbone's for the last thirty years or more. So when we submit a current version of a dish, it is just an example of how we are cooking at the restaurant presently. In respect to the past cooks and chefs of Carbone's, we make no claim of inventing the following dishes. We are, however, proud to offer the current evolution of them.

I offer special thanks to "Mama Jo" McKenzie, a true friend and the first lady of the Connecticut Restaurant Industry. She set premier standards with her own restaurants, the Copperbeach Inn and Robert Henry's.

Also, it has been a pleasure and an honor to work with Jane and Michael Stern. Thank you for your passion and patience in putting this book together along with Publisher Larry Stone and Editor Geoff Stone from Rutledge Hill Press.

— Vincent "Vinnie" Carbone

Acknowledgments

No restaurant is human, but a rare few have real character. That is particularly true of Carbone's, the charismatic personality of which is the expression of all those people who made it what it is and continue to uphold its values and traditions. Founders Charlie and Anthony Carbone as well as Angie Locario and Billie Carbone were there at the beginning, as was "Uncle" Roc LaCava. Charlie and Anthony are gone, but Angie, Billie, and Uncle Roc shared precious memories with us to help us understand what it was like to turn an empty lot into a thriving restaurant.

Guy Carbone and his son Vinnie now carry on and improve on their legacy, and they were boundlessly generous in sharing their time, knowledge, and enthusiasm as this book took shape.

This project would not have happened were it not for the tireless efforts of Mary-Beth Corraccio. Mary-Beth, who has been friends with Vinnie since grammar school and who has been part of Carbone's for the last twenty-five years, is the event coordinator for the restaurant and its catering operations. She is the person who gets things done when they need doing.

In addition, we are grateful to the Carbone's staff: Bar Manager Bob Brodeur, Sales Assistant Ann-Marie Brodeur, and Assistant Bar Manager Tommy Carbone. Co-Executive Chefs Paul Rafala and Michael McDowell fed us royally as we did our research; and we tip our hats to the brilliant work of Line Cooks Tony Scalise, Joe D'alesio, and John Sarkar, the Pastry Chef Angelo Famaglietti, the Baker Frankie Torres, and the Butcher Dino Diaz. As well, we salute the administrative and bookkeeping work of Lois Sonnone, Frances Corridino, and Clelia Carbone.

We offer special thanks and boundless admiration to "Mama Jo" McKenzie, bright light of Connecticut restaurants for so many years, special friend of Carbone's, and, for us, a true writer's muse.

As always, we are indebted to the world-class team at Rutledge Hill Press who make the creation of these Roadfood cookbooks such a pleasure: Publisher Larry Stone, Editor Geoff Stone, Marketing Director Brian Curtis, and Tracy Menges, who gets everything done. A special thanks to Idea Man (and eater) Extraordinaire Roger Waynick and his partner, Mike Alday.

Wherever we eat, our eating partners at www.roadfood.com accompany us, at least in spirit and appetite. Our Roadfood adventures have been so deeply enriched by our connection with Steve Rushmore Sr., Stephen Rushmore and Kristin Little, Cindy Keuchle, and Marc Bruno.

Last, but certainly not least, we thank our agent, Doe Coover, for taking such good care of us and Jean Wagner, Mary Ann Rudolph, and Ned Schankman for making it possible for us to travel in confidence that all's well at home.

Introduction

On the occasion of its thirty-fifth anniversary in 1973, Carbone's restaurant ran an advertisement in the *Hartford Courant* titled "Improving with Age." The ad noted that many contemporary dining establishments were streamlining menus and cutting back on service but that Carbone's would continue to do what had made it successful for so many years: ". . . offer dozens of entrées, prepare special dishes at your request, and cater to your every desire."

L to R: Original owners and brothers, Anthony Carbone and Charlie Carbone, Charlie's wife Frances, their sister Angie Locario, and Anthony's wife Billie.

Thirty years later, those principles have not changed. While much of the menu reflects modern interpretations of Italian regional cuisine and cutting-edge culinary style, this sixty-five-year-old treasure offers the tranquility of tradition. To settle into one of Carbone's thickly padded booths imparts a sense of stress-free déjà vu (even on your first visit). Family-run for three generations, Carbone's has perfected an intimacy that assures newcomers, as well as old friends, that they will be well taken care of. It is a deluxe establishment—arguably the suavest restaurant between Boston and New York—and yet its ambience is as comfortable as home, and its rituals of service induce an "all's-well-with-the-world" bliss. As you relax in the windowless dining room that keeps all thoughts of the humdrum world outside at bay, look around and appreciate the strength of the solid citizens who dine here with families or business associates: clergy, captains of industry, state representatives, and other people who come for a grand night on the town or simply to eat spectacularly well.

We have long believed that the Northeast has both the most and the finest Italian food in America, a match for anything you'd eat in Italy itself. In big cities such as Boston, Providence, and New York and in smaller ones stretching from Newark to New Haven to Northampton you can count on there being significant, deep-rooted Italian neighborhoods that will likely include salumerias (delis) and pork stores, gelaterias (ice cream shops) and pastry shops, brick-oven pizzerias, and at least one grand old family-run restaurant— of which Carbone's is the crème de la crème.

When it opened in 1938 Carbone's was the first restaurant in Hartford's South End, which was then a multicultural enclave of newly-arrived Jews, Germans, Poles, and Italians. Franklin

The original name of the restaurant advertised on a city bus.

Avenue later became known as Little Italy, and Carbone's was its culinary anchor. As a neighborhood bastion, Carbone's has been at the forefront of America's changing vision of what, exactly, Italian food is and what it ought to be. In the beginning, the restaurant was named the Southern Plantation because the family feared that an Italian name would discourage customers who thought of Italian food as crude peasant fare. Gradually, the family added more of their motherland's dishes to the menu, including sauce made by Mama Carbone in their home kitchen. Then in 1961, the restaurant went upscale and was renamed Carbone's.

It was a propitious time in culinary history to make the change, for the 1960s was a time when previously uninterested Americans were discovering gourmet food from around the world. Time-Life published a twenty-six volume series called *Foods of the World*, introducing the home cook to novel dishes that ranged from tempura shrimp to coq au vin. Restaurants that sought to take patrons on a delicious culinary tour of some

In 1949 the restaurant was called the Southern Plantation.

far-off part of the world opened in New York and elsewhere. One of the most conspicuous was the Forum of the Twelve Caesars, a hugely expensive theme restaurant where diners were treated like emperors and everything came from the kitchen with a flourish, enthroned on a rolling cart or impaled on a sword, and frequently set ablaze. This was a restaurant with an explicit Roman theme— hardly a spaghetti joint! The culinary statement made at the Forum was exactly what Gaetano and Carl Carbone wanted to say when they reformulated their own family restaurant: Italian food is a virtual treasury of taste that transcends the old cliché of soft-cooked, red-sauced noodles.

It was during the formative years of the new Carbone's that the food formerly known as macaroni became known as pasta. As John and Galina Mariani note about that era in their invaluable *Italian-American Cookbook*, "Red-checkered tablecloths and stucco were replaced with white linen and artfully mottled walls. Chianti-bottle candle holders gave way to Venetian glass sconces, and red waiters' jackets to black tuxedos."

Stylish tableside service was part of the new image at Carbone's, as was the presence of a serious chef in the kitchen. Gaetano Carbone, who had graduated from the Culinary Institute of America, printed up a different recipe every week for customers who yearned to try this kind of cooking at home. In his handouts, titled "The Master Presents," Guy was consciously educating his clientele in a fabulous Italianate cuisine that ranged from the now-familiar Fettuccini Alfredo to such exotica as Tagliatelle Verdi Con Cotechino di Maiale (green noodles with hog jowls) and Squid Anthony.

The menu has reached even further now that Guy's son Vincent runs the restaurant and executive chefs Mike McDowell and Paul Rafala create new dishes with him. The repertoire always includes such definitive Carbone's favorites as Veal Saltimbocca, Linguine Carbonara, and Sicilian Orange Salad, but it also extends to original dishes that are Italian-inspired, such as Chilean sea bass cooked with prosciutto and flavored with olive oil and balsamic vinegar. And while Vinnie spends most days as host in the front of the restaurant, he still gets to do the cooking that he loves in the go-anywhere Carbone's catering truck.

Vinnie Carbone showing off the mobile kitchen.

Because it is outfitted with a full kitchen, this truck means that when Carbone's caters a party at a home or business, no pre-cooked food is brought for reheating. Chef Vinnie cooks it right there, on the spot.

It is inspiring to look back and see how much the Carbone family restaurant and the gastronomic world around it have changed since the time Italian cuisine was so disparaged that they chose a distinctly non-Italian name.

Americans have discovered a delicious world beyond macaroni and red sauce. Playwright Neil Simon once commented, "There are two laws in the universe: The Law of Gravity and Everybody Likes Italian Food." As the Southern Plantation became Carbone's, it was a leading light in the growing love affair with the Italian kitchen. Today the meals it serves are both classic and cutting-edge, and its dining room remains one-of-a-kind.

L to R Bottom: Butcher Dino Diaz, Line Cook Joe D'Alesio, Baker Frankie Torres,
Line Cook John Sarkar
L to R Top: Co-Executive Chef Paul Rafala, Line Cook Tony Scalise, Guy Carbone,
Pastry Chef Angelo Famaglietti, Co-Executive Chef Michael McDowell

FROM GAS STATION TO GOURMET: THE CARBONE'S STORY

L to R: Anthony Carbone, son Tony Carbone, and brother Charlie Carbone

Times were lean in the 1930s when Charlie and Anthony Carbone ran an Atlantic Richfield gas station at the corner of Franklin Avenue and Goodrich Street in Hartford. The Great Depression had hit the building trade so badly that even though a foundation for an apartment building had been laid in a lot adjoining the Carbone's service station on the east side of Franklin Avenue, the building was never constructed. The builder could not raise the construction money. That vacant foundation inspired Carl (Charlie), Tony, and their sister Angie to begin dreaming about opening a restaurant on Hartford's South End, which was then a multiethnic community teeming with immigrants from nearly all of Europe's old countries.

The gas station was doing good business, but not enough to fund a restaurant. "In those days, we didn't believe in banks," recalls Billie Carbone, Anthony's wife. "So we borrowed our start-up money from a friend. And let me tell you, that money smelled! It smelled so bad. It was musty because he had squirreled it away for so long in his mattress or somewhere moldy."

The building went up, fixtures and secondhand furniture were bought on time-payment plans, and the restaurant opened. Tables and booths were covered with red-and-white checkered cloths; walls were paneled with knotty pine. In those days, few Americans without some Italian background

Inside the Southern Plantation Restuarant; Carbone's has come a long way.

appreciated Italian food, and a restaurant name that even suggested it was anathema. The Carbone family wanted to serve people from beyond the neighborhood. So they named their place the Southern Plantation, in part because it was on the South End, but also because an antebellum theme was more culturally acceptable than an Italian one. The menu consisted mostly of grinders—the local term for an Italian hero—and other sandwiches. Spaghetti with meatballs was added later, as were other pasta dishes, calzones, veal, roasts, and soups. A shot and a large beer were fifty cents. Local teens came in after school for sandwiches and Cokes and to watch the action at the bar, which included Charlie Carbone—a magician of sorts—doing card tricks.

"The prewar years had a quiet, family-type atmosphere," recalls "Uncle" Roc LaCava, a longtime friend of the Carbones and restaurant regular since he was seventeen years old. "Blue laws were in effect, which meant no standing at the bar on Sunday. Chairs were set up, which they called the 'Sunday chairs'—old school chairs with the flat area for writing. This is where drinks were served when you were not allowed at the bar."

Billie remembers that those early years were tough. "There were some times when we took in five dollars all day long," she said. "We'd bring money over from the gas station just to make change and keep going. We would try anything to attract customers," she said. "One year we had 'Dinner in May,' when if you bought one dinner, the second one cost a penny more. The next year it was two cents more." For a while, the Southern Plantation was Hartford's source for "Chicken in the Rough," a pre-KFC fried-chicken product that used an image of a golf-club-wielding chicken ("in the rough") as its mascot. "I got so darn tired of making biscuits," Billie laughed. "Biscuits and honey, biscuits and honey, sometimes it seemed like that's all there was to Chicken in the Rough."

Chicken in the Rough was the Southern Plantation's signature dish and Hartford's source for fried chicken.

In the beginning, none of the family working in the restaurant drew any pay at all. "Certainly not us girls!" Billie said emphatically. "Charlie and Tony thought women were there to work hard, and that was that. They were macho Italian men and felt that we women had little to say about the business, and let me tell you, that rankled us. My husband didn't even want to pay his sister Angie for bookkeeping. I blew my top over that!"

Carl and Anthony had learned some of what they knew about the restaurant trade from working at Hartford's fine old Bond Hotel, where owner Mr. Bond was known for his impeccably tight ship and Victorian standards. Tony once told a reporter, "The quickest way to lose your job is to let a woman smoke." At the Bond, if a waiter saw a woman light up, he was required to rush to her place and present her with a small card requesting that she immediately extinguish the cigarette. Also on this subject, it is interesting to note that Carbone's was the last place in Hartford to change its dress code to let women patrons wear pants. That was in 1970, when Charlie's sons finally prevailed upon their father by pointing out that even the Vatican allowed women visitors to wear pants.

Although spaghetti was added to the menu, the Southern Plantation was far from the definitive Italian restaurant it finally became. For a while it was a kind of prototypical "sports bar" across from the old Bulkeley Stadium, which was home to summer motorcycle races and then, starting the same year the family opened the restaurant, to baseball games of the Hartford Chiefs, a Boston Braves farm club. Ballplayers came in for sandwiches and beer long into the night; and after games the place was mobbed with fans. "We'd run out of dessert some nights," Billie recalls. "I'd find myself making chiffon pies at eleven or midnight."

Charlie yearned to serve more than sandwiches and spaghetti with beer; he wanted his place to be a showcase for the Italian food he knew from his family (some of whom were from south Italy, some from the north). In the 1940s the kitchen expanded and chefs were hired. "But Charlie couldn't get any of them to do things his way," said Angie Locario, Charlie's sister. "So they came and they went, and Charlie took over. He had a vision of how he wanted the restaurant to be, and no one else could fulfill that. He introduced Italian food dish by dish, first one and then another added to the menu."

Help was nearly impossible to find during World War II, and all Carbones who weren't in the armed services pitched in. Children washed dishes, then graduated to busing tables. Angie was the bookkeeper, Billie and Frances baked, Anthony's job was to make the dining room a showcase of hospitality, and Charlie Sr. ran the kitchen.

Uncle Roc recalls that the end of the war was especially festive. "We had all gone into the service and served in the world's battlefields," he said. "At the end, boys were coming home by twos and threes every month. And homecoming meant that it was another time for drinking and for partying. This went on for the whole year of 1946. When Charlie Carbone returned from the navy, the party at the restaurant lasted three days."

The secrets behind the success: handwritten Carbone family recipes.

During the postwar years Charlie and Anthony both returned to Italy to refresh their taste buds; and Charlie frequently went down to New York to see what the Italian restaurants were cooking. There were some chefs who welcomed him into their kitchens and shared their recipes. Other times, he employed guile to find out what he needed to know. In one Manhattan establishment, he posed as an inspector from the health department and insisted that he be shown around the kitchen to see if they were preparing their food according to department standards. All the while he took notes that the restaurateurs and chefs assumed regarded health standards. In fact, Charlie was deciphering recipes as he watched dishes being prepared.

In the spring of 1961, with Charlie's son Gaetano (Guy) fresh out of the Culinary Institute of America and another son, Carl, graduated from the Hotel and Restaurant Management program of the State University of New York, the family restaurant underwent a dramatic change. The Southern Plantation became history. Carbone's was born. The family-style, low-price sandwich and spaghetti *trattoria* was transformed into an aspiring Italian *ristorante* with deluxe red and white Mediterranean décor that included wrought iron chandeliers and elegant high-backed chairs as well as ultracapacious tufted booths suitable for high-power business lunches and special-occasion family dinners. A serious wine list was established and the menu expanded to include specialties from throughout Italy. "It was a most appropriate time to specialize," Carl Jr. commented. "The public was becoming gourmet-minded."

During the era that Uncle Roc describes as "the glory days of the restaurant," Carl and Guy introduced the practice of wheeling food on carts

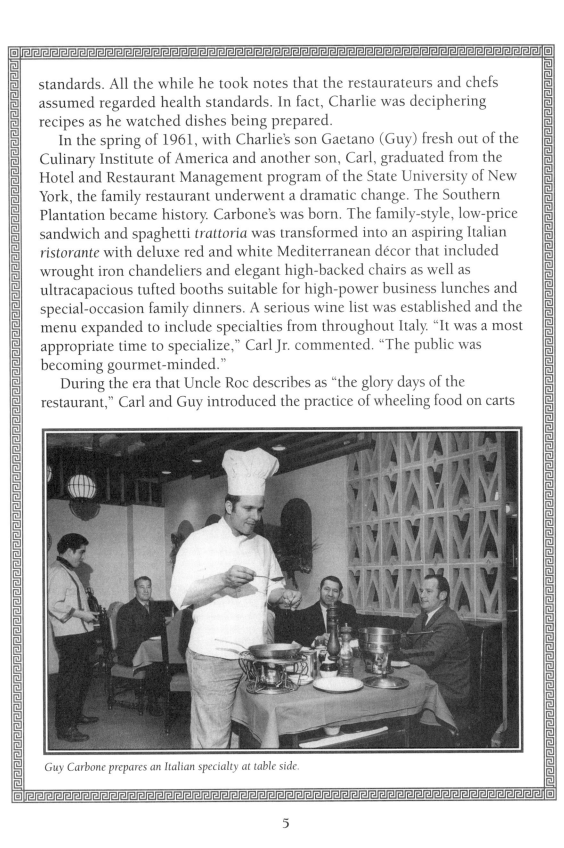

Guy Carbone prepares an Italian specialty at table side.

to customers and including tableside pyrotechnics as part of the dining experience.

"From grinders to gourmet" is Uncle Roc's description of Carbone's evolution. In the decades since that transformation, the place that began as a sandwich shop next to a gas station has enjoyed amazing longevity. Its well-being stems in part from the fact that in a very important sense, it never changed. It is today what it was from the very beginning: a family affair. Gaetano, whose son Vincent now runs the place, recalls that "you could always find a dozen or more family members working on Saturday evenings or on special-occasion nights such as New Year's Eve and Valentine's Day. We cooked, managed, tended bar, hosted, served, bused, washed dishes, and took coats for the cloakroom. Saturday mornings and afternoons, the restaurant was always filled with at least twelve children either scrubbing the hoods in the kitchen or polishing the silver."

Nearly twenty years ago, a reviewer in *Connecticut Magazine* noted that the annual readers' poll had selected Carbone's as the state's favorite Italian restaurant "for as long as man can remember." It has consistently retained that position into the twenty-first century.

· SOUPS & SALADS ·

(Zuppe e Insalate)

Chickpea Soup
Bean-Escarole Soup
Lentil Soup
Beef Stock
Chicken Stock
Vegetable Soup
Fish Stock

• • •

Caesar Salad
Tomato Salad
Gorgonzola Salad
Orange Salad
Spinach Salad
Pear and Gorgonzola Salad
Tuna Salad
Roasted Beet and Goat Cheese Salad
Arugula Salad
Cold Seafood Salad

Zuppa di Ceci

(CHICKPEA SOUP)

While chickpea soup is usually offered in small portions as an appetizer in the restaurant, it also makes a hearty, one-bowl meal. It's an economical dish that was originally made from whatever groceries the cook had on hand.

1	pound chickpeas
2	tablespoons olive oil
2	tablespoons diced salt pork
1	clove garlic
¾	cup diced onions
½	cup crushed tomatoes
6	plus 6 cups chicken stock
1	bay leaf
	Salt and pepper
1¼	cup tubetini macaroni

Soak the chickpeas overnight. Heat the oil and salt pork in a soup pot over medium heat. Add the garlic until it browns; discard the garlic. Add the diced onions and tomatoes; sauté for 5 minutes. Add 6 cups of chicken stock, the chickpeas, bay leaf, and salt and pepper to taste. Cook for 4 hours or more over low heat. Add the rest of the chicken stock as some evaporates. Meanwhile, cook the tubetini according to the package directions and add it to the soup.

MAKES 10 TO 12 SERVINGS

Escarola Fagioli
(BEAN-ESCAROLE SOUP)

A year-round soup using the Italian cook's favorite bitter green, escarole. "Here is an example of the fundamentally well-balanced nature of Italian cooking," Vinnie points out.

1	pound dry white beans
½	cup olive oil
1	clove garlic
1	cup diced onions
1	tomato, chopped
12	cups (3 quarts) chicken stock
1	head escarole, washed and chopped
	Salt and pepper
	Grated Ramano cheese

Soak the beans overnight. Heat the oil in a saucepan and brown the garlic; discard the garlic. Add the onions and sauté for 5 minutes. Add the tomato, chicken stock, and beans and simmer for 2½ hours. Add the escarole and salt and pepper to taste. Cook for another 20 minutes. Top each serving bowl with grated cheese.

MAKES 10 TO 12 SERVINGS

Zuppa di Lenticchia
(LENTIL SOUP)

Lentils were a change from beans," Vinnie says about this robust soup, which he calls a good example of the frugality of Italian cooks. "You used what you had; and most of the time, what you had were dried things in the cupboard, things that wouldn't spoil."

1	*pound lentils*
3	*tablespoons olive oil*
2	*cloves garlic*
¼	*cup diced carrots*
¼	*cup celery*
¼	*cup diced onions*
½	*cup crushed tomatoes*
12	*cups (3 quarts) beef stock*
	Salt and pepper
½	*cup cooked pasta (optional)*

Soak the lentils overnight. Heat the oil in a saucepan and brown the garlic; discard the garlic. Sauté the carrots, celery, and onions for 5 minutes. Add the tomatoes, lentils, and beef stock and simmer until tender, or about 1 hour. Salt and pepper to taste. If pasta is desired, add ½ cup cooked pasta. Before serving you may add a dash of olive oil to each cup of soup.

MAKES 10 TO 12 SERVINGS

Note: Cooked fresh spinach may be served in this soup for variety.

Brodo di Manzo

(BEEF STOCK)

Beef stock is made from bones and scraps after the better cuts are used for other dishes. It can be prepared in advance and frozen to have on hand whenever you need its full-flavored character in a dish.

4	pounds beef bones (shank)
2	pounds lean beef
20	cups (5 quarts) plus 1 cup cold water
½	cup red wine
2	stalks celery
2	carrots
1	onion
1	teaspoon tomato paste
1	teaspoon salt
	Ground black pepper
1	bouquet garni*

Preheat the oven to 400°F. Brown the bones and beef for 30 minutes in the oven to produce color and flavor. Put the meat and bones in a stockpot with the 5 quarts cold water. Bring to a boil and reduce the heat to a simmer, skimming off the foam and fat. Deglaze the roasting pan with the wine and 1 cup water. (Cook over high heat on top of the stove until the liquid is reduced by half.) Add this to the stock. Add the celery, carrots, and onion whole. Add the teaspoon salt and black pepper to taste. Add the bouquet garni and cook for 3 to 4 hours. Remove from the heat and strain through a cheesecloth. Remove the fat that forms on top.

MAKES 5 QUARTS (10 TO 12 SERVINGS)

*A bouquet garni is a combination of fresh and dry herbs tied together in cheesecloth, added to the stock, and removed when done. Use fresh thyme, 2 bay leaves, 3 cloves garlic, and ½ bunch of Italian parsley.

Brodo di Pollo

(CHICKEN STOCK)

Good chicken stock traditionally is made from whatever parts of a bird are left from preparing other dishes. The original recipe calls for fowl, and in fact an old-fashioned stewing hen (hard to find in markets these days), too tough for most entrées, makes the most full-flavored stock.

4	to 5 pounds chicken
1	pound chicken necks and backs
20	cups (5 quarts) water
1	stalk celery
1	carrot
1	onion
1	whole tomato
1	teaspoon salt
1	bouquet garni*

Put chicken; necks, and backs in a stockpot with the cold water. Bring to a boil and reduce the heat to a simmer, skimming off the fat and foam. Add the celery, carrot, and onion whole. Add the whole tomato, salt, and bouquet garni and cook over medium heat for 3 hours. Remove from the heat and strain through cheesecloth. Remove the fat that forms on top.

MAKES 5 QUARTS (10 TO 12 SERVINGS)

*A bouquet garni is a combination of fresh and dry herbs tied together in cheesecloth, added to the stock and removed when done. Use fresh thyme, 2 bay leaves, 3 cloves garlic, and ½ bunch of Italian parsley.

Minestrone

(VEGETABLE SOUP)

Charlie Carbone was a soup man. "He would live on soups during Lent," Guy remembers. "We kids would go crazy because we didn't want to give up meat."

¼	cup diced salt pork
¼	cup olive oil
2	cloves garlic
1	cup chopped celery
1	cup chopped onion
1	cup chopped carrots
½	head cabbage, shredded
1	cup diced tomatoes
12	cups (3 quarts) beef stock (see page 12)
½	cup tubetini macaroni
1	cup cooked chickpeas
	Salt and pepper
	Parmesan cheese

Cook the salt pork in oil; add the garlic and brown. Discard the garlic. Add the celery, onion, carrots, and cabbage to the pot. Sauté over medium heat for 15 minutes. Add the tomatoes and beef stock and cook gently on low for 15 minutes. Add the pasta and chickpeas and cook over low heat for 10 minutes. Salt and pepper to taste. Top with Parmesan cheese.

MAKES 10 TO 12 SERVINGS

Brodo di Pesce

(FISH STOCK)

Vinnie told us that the prudent Italian cook always saves the trimmings from a fish dish to use as the base for fish stock. This stock can then be used to make soups and sauces.

1	small onion, chopped
¼	cup chopped celery
¼	cup chopped carrots
3	tablespoons butter
	Juice of 1 lemon
¼	cup Marsala wine
3	pounds fish trimmings
1	gallon water
1	bouquet garni*

Sauté over medium heat the onion, celery, and carrots in the butter for 5 minutes. Add the lemon juice and Marsala wine. Stir the ingredients, cover, and simmer for 10 minutes. Add the fish trimmings, water, and bouquet garni. Bring to a boil and then simmer for 45 minutes, covered. Strain through a fine sieve.

MAKES 10 TO 12 SERVINGS

* A bouquet garni is a combination of fresh and dry herbs tied together in cheesecloth, added to the stock and removed when done. Use 1 bay leaf, 1 teaspoon thyme, ½ bunch parsley, and 6 crushed peppercorns.

SALADS

Salads are not secondary side dishes at Carbone's. The lunchtime Caesar salad, available topped with the kitchen's incomparable fried calamari, is a bravura meal. Starting in the early 1960s, the making and serving of fabulous salads became a hallmark of the dining room. Preparation of salads at customers' tables included consultation between guest and waiter as to the diners' exact preferences regarding seasoning, as well as the strict practice of tossing the lettuce in custom-flavored oil and vinegar dressing exactly seven times. "The most important thing to do when making a salad is to coat the leaves with oil first," Carl Carbone told a newspaper reporter in 1974. "That way the seasonings will adhere to the leaves and enhance the flavor."

Spinach salad, quickly flambéed to give a light glow of warmth, is among the showstoppers on the menu. The best known is the Sicilian Orange Salad, a creation described in a 1980s nationally syndicated newspaper story as "a tableside production number, beginning vaguely like Caesar salad, but then veering away from cheese and romaine lettuce to incorporate the Sicilian citrus bounty." The Sicilian salad is so well-known to regular customers that it is not even listed on the menu!

Insalata Cesare

(CAESAR SALAD)

Named for the Roman emperor and a staple in virtually every Italian-American restaurant, Caesar salad was in fact invented in Tijuana, Mexico, in the 1920s. Classic versions call for whole leaves of lettuce, and proper dining etiquette says the leaves may be picked up in one's fingers. Carbone's version is the more familiar version, with bite-size shreds of Romaine . . . to be eaten with a fork.

2	heads romaine lettuce
½	cup olive oil
4	anchovy fillets, finely chopped
2	cloves garlic, chopped
3	tablespoons vinegar
	Dash of Worcestershire sauce
2	to 3 drops Tabasco sauce
1½	teaspoons dry mustard
2	egg yokes, beaten
½	cup grated Romano cheese
1	cup croutons
	Salt and pepper

Thoroughly wash the romaine lettuce. Tear it into pieces and chill. Blend the anchovies and garlic in oil. In another bowl combine the vinegar, Worcestershire sauce, Tabasco, mustard, and egg yokes. Add the anchovies and garlic. Toss the dressing with the romaine lettuce. Sprinkle cheese and croutons on top. Season with salt and pepper to taste.

MAKES 6 SERVINGS

Insalata di Pomodoro

(TOMATO SALAD)

You can make this salad year-round, but the best time is late summer when tomatoes with real tomato flavor ripen on the vine. It wasn't so long ago that it was common to see tomato plants growing in the yards of people who lived in Hartford's South End.

5	*medium-size ripe tomatoes, quartered*
1	*medium-size onion, sliced*
1	*green pepper, sliced*
¼	*cup olive oil*
1	*teaspoon oregano*
4	*fresh basil leaves, torn into pieces*
	Salt and freshly ground pepper

Place the tomatoes, onion, and pepper in a bowl. Add the oil, oregano, basil, and salt and pepper to taste; toss lightly until thoroughly mixed. Chill before serving.

MAKES 4 TO 6 SERVINGS

Insalata di Lattuga al Gorgonzola

(GORGONZOLA SALAD)

Authentic Gorgonzola cheese comes from northern Italy and is named for the town that makes it. But even true Gorgonzola cheese varies in character from smooth and mild to salty and sharp. For this salad, you want one with assertive taste and creamy texture.

1	head romaine lettuce
3	tablespoons olive oil
2	tablespoons grated Romano cheese
2	tablespoons wine vinegar
¼	cup Gorgonzola cheese
¼	teaspoon dry mustard
½	teaspoon Worcestershire sauce
	Salt and pepper

Thoroughly wash and drain the romaine lettuce. Cut it into pieces and place it in a bowl. Toss the lettuce with the oil. In a small bowl thoroughly blend the Romano cheese, vinegar, Gorgonzola cheese, mustard, and Worcestershire sauce. Pour the mixture over the salad and season with salt and pepper to taste.

MAKES 4 TO 6 SERVINGS

Insalata all' Arancia

(ORANGE SALAD)

The traditional role of salad on the Italian table is as a minor intermezzo between the meal and dessert. At Carbone's, salad is hardly a minor event. The making and serving of salads has become one of the restaurant's beloved rituals; and this orange salad—which is Sicilian by ancestry—is one of the favorites.

6	*large oranges*
1	*small onion*
4	*anchovy fillets*
1	*clove garlic*
6	*tablespoons oil*
	Juice of ½ lemon
1	*teaspoon mustard*
	Hot pepper seeds
	Salt and pepper
1	*teaspoon chopped parsley*

Peel the oranges. Slice and arrange them on a cold platter. Thinly slice the onion and arrange it over the oranges. Crush the anchovies and garlic; add the oil, lemon juice, and mustard and blend. Sprinkle the pepper seeds over the oranges and salt and pepper to taste. Sprinkle the parsley over the oranges. Spoon the anchovy sauce on the oranges and serve.

MAKES 6 SERVINGS

Insalata di Spinaci

(SPINACH SALAD)

Spinach salad is one of the longtime signature dishes of Carbone's dining room, traditionally prepared tableside with a great flaming detonation to mark the completion of the warm dressing. The pyrotechnics are more for show than flavor, so we recommend that you not ignite this salad at home. Merely heat the oil.

12	*to 16 ounces fresh spinach*
1	*cup sliced raw mushrooms*
4	*slices Bermuda onion*
½	*cup plus 1 tablespoon olive oil*
¼	*cup vinegar*
1	*to 2 teaspoons sugar*
	Salt and pepper
½	*cup crisply cooked and chopped bacon*

Wash the spinach leaves thoroughly and remove all dark spots. Use only the young and tender leaves. Toss the spinach, mushrooms, and onion with 1 tablespoon olive oil. Heat the remaining ½ cup of olive oil in a small frying pan until warm and put aside. To the spinach add the vinegar, sugar, and salt and pepper to taste and toss lightly. Pour on the warm olive oil and sprinkle the bacon pieces on top of the salad before serving.

MAKES 6 TO 8 SERVINGS

TABLESIDE FIREWORKS

It is possible to have an intimate, sequestered meal at Carbone's in what feels like a quiet booth all your own. But for many customers, coming to Carbone's means dinner and a show. The preparation of flaming dishes at the table provides the show. Meals literally glow—from spinach salad that goes "poof" as its olive-oil dressing is ignited, to the globe of chocolate-covered ice cream enrobed in flaming liqueur in the "bocce ball" dessert. Carbone's has been known for tableside pyrotechnics since it remodeled and reopened in 1961 as an Italian restaurant with something extra—cooking with an open flame was exotic and seductive. *The Pyromaniac's Cookbook,* published later in the 1960s, explained that flambéed foods appeal to the senses as well as the intellect; they are at once primitive and the height of culinary sophistication. The restaurant that originally popularized flaming rites, in the 1950s, was Newark Airport's Newarker, one of the first successful dining-as-entertainment ventures by Restaurant Associates. *Gourmet* magazine praised the Newarker for "flaming foods in all their glory," referring to such showy preparation as a "magic ingredient."

To watch the ceremony—Linguine Carbonara mixed and heated and set on fire—is enjoyable; but beyond the entertainment value, this kind of service provides assurance that the food being placed in front of you was prepared only seconds earlier. In 1971 reviewer Cynthia Lang marveled at the extremely personalized nature of the dining experience at Carbone's. "Everything is prepared for you," she wrote, describing the restaurant as an instrument in fine tune, and the flambé service in particular as pleasurable, adventuresome, and romantic.

Guy Carbone himself continues the tradition of culinary showmanship he began, although his son Vinnie now runs the show, and it is the waitstaff who does the everyday flaming of pasta dishes, desserts, and specialty coffees. Wednesdays in the bar Guy sets up a couple of rolling carts and burners, and whatever ingredients he needs to prepare a flamboyant lunchtime special. By midday, the U-shaped counter of the bar is set with fifteen settings of silverware and white napkins, and about noon, a group of Carbone's regulars starts gathering at their usual places. (On days when there are more of these friends than there are seats, they take turns.) Once most of the crew is assembled, each tells bar manager Bob Brodeur that he or she wants the day's special. Bob calls out to Guy, "Seven Steak Dianes . . . no, make that nine . . . no, eleven!" Guy goes to work whipping up the main course as Vinnie helps him by getting plates ready with vegetables. Meanwhile, the folks at the bar are having their beverages along with baskets of just-fried potato chips and are vociferously discussing the political and sports issues of the day.

Guy Carbone preparing the famous Steak Diane, or three.

Insalata di Gorgonzola e Pera

(PEAR AND GORGONZOLA SALAD)

Sweet, slightly grainy-textured pears and creamy-sharp cheese combine to give this salad a rainbow flavor, enriched by walnuts and walnut oil.

½	cup walnut oil
¼	cup sherry wine vinegar
1	tablespoon Dijon mustard
4	heads of frisée, washed and separated by hand
1	teaspoon chopped garlic
8	ounces (½ cup) Gorgonzola cheese, crumbled
2	Anjou pears, seeded and sliced
¼	cup chopped walnuts

Blend the walnut oil, vinegar, and mustard together to create an emulsion. Toss with the frisée, chopped garlic, and Gorgonzola cheese. Garnish with sliced pears and walnuts.

MAKES 4 SERVINGS

Insalata Tonno

(TUNA SALAD)

Do not under any circumstances think of using fresh tuna in this salad. Its character depends on canned tuna—good canned tuna, packed in olive oil.

1	pound mesclun greens
10	medium kalamata olives, pitted and chopped
	Juice of 2 lemons, divided in half
¼	cup feta cheese
¼	plus ¼ cup olive oil
12	ounces Tongol tuna, drained
½	ounce capers
½	red onion, chopped
2	teaspoons chopped fresh parsley
1	teaspoon ground black pepper
12	grape tomatoes

In a bowl mix the mesclun greens, olives, half the lemon juice, feta, and ¼ cup olive oil. In a separate bowl, mix the tuna, capers, onion, parsley, and black pepper with the other half of the lemon juice, feta, and remaining oil. Divide the salad onto four plates. Top with the tuna mixture; garnish evenly with the grape tomatoes.

MAKES 4 SERVINGS

Insalata di Capra

(ROASTED BEET AND GOAT CHEESE SALAD)

It is some effort to prepare this salad, but it is a showstopper. The small spheres of goat cheese have a creamy center that sings beautiful harmony with roasted beets.

2	large beets
½	plus ½ plus ¼ cups olive oil
⅓	cup rice wine vinegar
1	teaspoon Dijon mustard
1	teaspoon Worcestershire sauce
1	teaspoon salt
1	teaspoon black pepper
1	teaspoon chopped garlic
¼	cup all-purpose flour
2	eggs, beaten
½	cup Panko breadcrumbs
8	ounces goat cheese
1	head romaine, washed and chopped
1	head iceberg, washed and chopped
1	head radicchio, washed and chopped

Preheat the oven to 300°F. Place the beets in a roasting pan with ¼ cup of olive oil. Roast the beets until brown, about 30 minutes. Cover the pan and continue roasting the beets for 2 hours, or until tender. In a blender place 1 beet, ½ cup olive oil, the rice wine vinegar, mustard, Worcestershire sauce, salt, pepper, and garlic; blend until emulsified. Put the flour, eggs, and breadcrumbs in separate bowls. In a 1-quart pot heat the remaining ½ cup olive oil over medium-high heat. Form the goat cheese into eight small balls. Dredge each cheese ball in the flour, then the egg, and then the breadcrumbs. Deep-fry the balls in the heated oil until golden brown. Remove from the oil when done. Divide the lettuces among four plates, making a bed on each plate. Slice the remaining beet and divide it among the plates on top of the lettuce. Drizzle the vinaigrette dressing over the beet and lettuce and garnish with the goat cheese balls.

MAKES 4 SERVINGS

Insalata Arugula

(ARUGULA SALAD)

For this salad you want the most tender leaves of arugula and the thinnest sliced prosciutto and cheese. The delicate textures belie the powerhouse punch of the ingredients' flavors.

½	cup olive oil
	Juice of 2 lemons
6	cloves garlic, peeled and thinly sliced
½	teaspoon black pepper
1	pound baby arugula
¼	pound prosciutto di Parma (approximately 8 slices)
4	ounces Parmigiano-Reggiano cheese, shaved

Mix together the olive oil, lemon, garlic, and pepper. Toss the dressing with the arugula. Line four plates with 2 slices prosciutto di Parma, and then divide the arugula among the plates on top of the prosciutto. Garnish each salad with the shaved Parmigiano-Reggiano cheese.

MAKES 4 SERVINGS

Insalata Frutti di Mare

(COLD SEAFOOD SALAD)

This one is a specialty of Angie Locario, sister of founders Charlie and Anthony Carbone. Aunt Angie frequently added scungilli to the mix.

SALAD:

8	ounces extra large shrimp
8	ounces fresh tuna, cubed in ½ inch pieces
16	mussels, steamed then removed from shell
8	ounces crabmeat, prepared
1	head Bibb lettuce
20	ounces Chef's Dressing (see below)

GARNISH:

4	eggs, hard-cooked
	Kalamata olives
	Lemon wedges

CHEF'S DRESSING:

1½	cups French dressing
1¼	cups mayonnaise
2	tablespoons Worcestershire sauce
2	tablespoons chopped parsley
2	tablespoons chopped fresh tarragon
2	tablespoons minced shallots
½	teaspoon curry powder
½	teaspoon cumin
2	tablespoons horseradish
	Juice of ½ lemon
	Salt and pepper

Boil the shrimp in water for about 5 minutes. Grill the tuna on a hot grill for about 1 minute per side. Set aside. Steam the mussels until the shells open, about 5 minutes. Remove the fish from the shell.

To make the Chef's Dressing, in a bowl whip together the French dressing, mayonnaise, Worcestershire sauce, parsley, tarragon, shallots, curry powder, cumin, horseradish, lemon juice, and salt and pepper to taste.

To make the salad, in a bowl combine the shrimp, tuna, mussels, and crabmeat and mix with the dressing. Chill for ½ hour. Divide the Bibb lettuce among four salad plates, making a bed. Portion the chilled seafood over the beds of lettuce. Garnish the dish with the eggs—eggs should be cut lengthwise in four pieces—olives, and lemon wedges.

MAKES 4 SERVINGS

· APPETIZERS ·

(Antipasti)

Marinated Tenderloin of Beef Carpaccio
Sausage and White Bean Dip for Bruschetta
Black Mission Figs with Mozzarella and Prosciutto
Chicken Skewers LaCava
Cheese Fondue
Fried Eggplant
Fried Calamari
Sicilian Stuffed Peppers
Cheese in Carriage
Spinach Pie Nicola
Sicilian Relish
Italian Ham and Melon
Clams Casino
Baked Stuffed Clams
Mussels in Tomato Sauce
Stuffed Mushrooms
Roasted Garlic

Carpaccio di Manzo

(MARINATED TENDERLOIN OF BEEF CARPACCIO)

Carbone's carpaccio is sliced so thinly you can read through it; and it is presented on crisp bona chutes of peasant bread. On the side come dressed wild greens and chilled béarnaise or tarragon aïoli sauce.

	MARINADE:		
3	to 4 anchovy fillets	3	to 4 (10 to 14 leaves) sprigs thyme
½	cup whole garlic cloves, peeled	3	to 4 (10 to 14 leaves) sprigs rosemary
½	cup whole black peppercorns		
¼	cup Japanese sea salt or kosher salt		Extra virgin olive oil (best quality)
¼	cup soy sauce		
¼	cup lemon-infused olive oil	1	pound center-cut, prime beef tenderloin (may use choice if prime is unavailable)
¼	cup hot-pepper-infused olive oil		
3	to 4 (10 to 14 leaves) sprigs fresh basil		Peasant bread (or other crusty bread)
3	to 4 (10 to 14 leaves) sprigs oregano		

To make the marinade, in a food processor combine the anchovies, garlic cloves, peppercorns, salt, soy sauce, lemon-infused olive oil, hot-pepper-infused olive oil, basil, oregano, thyme, and rosemary. Grind the mixture for at least 5 minutes, or until the peppercorns are completely crushed. Add extra virgin olive oil as you go to keep the mixture moist.

Massage the marinade onto the tenderloin for 10 minutes or so, trying to get all the mix onto the beef. Roll the tenderloin in plastic wrap so it forms a tight seal and refrigerate it for at least 4 hours (8 to 12 hours is better).

To serve the carpaccio, slice the beef paper-thin (so you can read through it) and place the slices on very thin, crispy bona chutes of peasant bread.

MAKES 4 TO 6 SERVINGS

31

Bruschetta con Salsiccia e Fagioli

(SAUSAGE AND WHITE BEAN DIP FOR BRUSCHETTA)

Bruschettas of all kinds have gained tremendous popularity in America's Italian restaurants. Like pizza, their toppings range from the simplest tomato and cheese to virtual whole meals atop the toasted bread. Sausage and white beans is a classic Italian combination; and in this dish, they are served with rather than atop the toast.

3	*plus 3 tablespoons extra virgin olive oil*
4	*ounces (sweet or hot) Italian-style sausage, out of the casing*
8	*ounces dried cannellini beans (white kidney)*
4	*to 6 garlic cloves, roasted*
2	*tablespoons (3 to 4 leaves) chopped fresh basil*
1	*to 2 cups diced potatoes, roasted or cooked*
½	*cup beef stock*
2	*to 4 ounces mixed greens* (a good handful or two)*
	Salt and freshly ground pepper

Over medium heat, put 3 tablespoons olive oil in a sauté pan (do not use a nonstick pan for this), add the sausage, and break it into small pieces while it is cooking. When the sausage is about two-thirds done, add the beans, roasted garlic, basil, potatoes, and beef stock. Turn the temperature to low and finish cooking the sausage in the broth, making sure not to boil out all the liquid. When the sausage is done, mix in the greens and cook until they're wilted but not mushy. Season with salt and pepper to taste. Transfer the sausage and beans to plates and finish by dividing the remaining olive oil over each serving. Accompany with toasted, sliced Italian bread.

MAKES 2 TO 4 SERVINGS

*Note: The greens we use in the restaurant vary greatly from dish to dish. The combination of the mix (i.e. bitter, sweet, mustard) is targeted for the outcome of the dish. There are prepared mixes available, or you can make your own. A nice variation is to use a single heavier green like broccoli raab or escarole.

Fichi con Mozzarella Fresca e Prosciutto di Parma

(BLACK MISSION FIGS WITH FRESH MOZZARELLA AND PROSCIUTTO DI PARMA)

Look for fresh figs that are tender but not squishy. The combination of their fruity sweetness and the salty smack of prosciutto is powerfully addictive . . . so much so that these are too much of a great appetizer before a big meal. With cocktails or as the prelude to something light, though, they're spectacular.

2	*fresh black mission figs, halved*
4	*slices fresh buffalo mozzarella cheese*
4	*fresh basil or mint leaves*
4	*slices prosciutto di Parma*

For each wrap, place a fig half, mozzarella slice, and basil or mint leaf on a slice of prosciutto di Parma. Roll the prosciutto slice. Repeat the steps with the remaining ingredients and serve the wraps on a bed of mixed wild greens on the cool side, but not "out-of-the-fridge" cold.

MAKES 4 SERVINGS

Note: Basil-infused lemon oil or mint-infused olive oil sprinkled on top adds a nice flavor to the appetizer.

LITTLE ITALY

"Uncle" Roc LaCava is an honorary Carbone. He was seventeen years old when the restaurant opened in 1938, and he has been close to it, and to the family, ever since. He reminisced about life along the streets of the Italian part of town in the years before World War II:

> The people of Front Street considered themselves as an independent area of Hartford, known as the East Side. It was a busy, noisy place. Pushcarts lined the streets, where people haggled over prices. Loud music came from the apartments—mostly the classics or the popular singers of the time. Many stores displayed their goods hanging from the ceiling—prosciutto, pepperoni, salami, provolone cheeses—and along the wall were barrels of chestnuts.

From the Italian neighborhood of Front Street, many residents began to move away from the city towards Wethersfield and Franklin Avenue. At the time, Franklin Avenue was a polyglot place with immigrants from all over Europe; but by the postwar years it was mostly Italian. "One of the fall rituals on Franklin Avenue was the wine-making," Uncle Roc recalls. "This turned into a neighborhood affair—helping each other with the grinding and the pressing of the grapes. Empty grape boxes could be seen stacked all along the avenue.

"When the wine was ready to taste, many a loud debate took place as to who made the best. No one ever won these debates, but after a while, no one cared. A great time was had by all."

Pollo allo Spiedino LaCava

(CHICKEN SKEWERS LaCAVA)

When you step into Carbone's restaurant, even today, you might meet Uncle Roc LaCava, who has been with the place as long as any blood-member of the family. Uncle Roc is a man of simple taste; and these skewers of chicken, while not spectacular to look at, are the most-requested hors d'oeuvre at Carbone's year after year.

½	*skinless, boneless chicken breast, cut into small bite-size pieces*
1	*cup seasoned breadcrumbs*
6	*slices bacon, cut in half*
3	*large hot stuffed cherry peppers*, quartered*
12	*toothpicks or bamboo skewers*

In a bowl combine the chicken pieces and breadcrumbs. Lay out the bacon side by side. On each piece of bacon place a piece of breaded chicken and a hot stuffed cherry pepper quarter. Roll the bacon around the chicken and pepper and then skewer it with a toothpick or bamboo skewer. You can either fry or bake the skewers. To fry the skewers, fill a heavy saucepot with vegetable oil (about 4 inches from the bottom) and heat it on the stove to 350°F, keeping a thermometer in the oil at all times to prevent overheating and ignition of the oil. When the oil achieves a constant temperature cook the skewers until golden brown, about 2 minutes. To bake the skewers, preheat the oven to 350°F, put them on a baking sheet, and bake until they are cooked through, about 5 minutes. They will not be crispy this way unless you burn them.

MAKES 12 SERVINGS

*Note: The hot stuffed cherry peppers we use are now a common brand and can be found in most Italian markets or the "ethnic" section of your local supermarket.

Fonduta di Formaggio

(CHEESE FONDUE)

Italian fondue" is how Vinnie Carbone describes this appetizer, customarily served in a hollowed-out loaf of the restaurant's delicious peasant bread. "There's a great contrast of flavors: the bresaola, the cheese, and the pear." It's a winter dish that's especially sociable at cocktail hour.

2	tablespoons softened butter
2	tablespoons chopped garlic
1	loaf crusty round bread (4 inches in diameter)
4	ounces Ashe goat cheese
4	ounces Stilton cheese (blue cheese)
⅛	cup chopped walnuts
3	paper-thin slices bresaola or prosciutto di Parma
1	Anjou pear
	Frisée, chopped
	Virgin olive oil

Preheat the oven to 300°F. Mix together the butter and garlic. Rub the outsides of the bread with the butter/garlic mixture and bake for 5 minutes. Remove the bread, cut a 2-inch hole in the top, and pull out the middle, forming a bowl. Melt the goat cheese and Stilton cheese together in a double boiler over low heat. Mix in the walnuts. Line the bottom of a 6-inch pie plate with three slices of bresaola. Cut the pear into six slices and place two slices on each piece of beef. Place the bread bowl in the center of the plate and fill it with the melted cheese mixture. Garnish the plate by placing the chopped frisée drizzled with virgin olive oil in between the pear slices.

MAKES 2 SERVINGS

Melanzane Fritto

(FRIED EGGPLANT)

It is almost impossible to conceive of serving fried eggplant without plenty of libations. As munchable as potato chips, these crisp, salty sticks may be served with or without tomato sauce for dipping.

1	*large eggplant*
½	*teaspoon salt*
½	*teaspoon pepper*
1	*cup flour*
2	*eggs, beaten*
2	*tablespoons milk*
1½	*cups cracker meal*
	Vegetable oil
	Seasoned salt
2	*tablespoons grated Parmesan cheese*

Peel and julienne the eggplant. Combine the salt, pepper, and flour. Mix together the egg and milk. Dust the eggplant strips with the seasoned flour and dip them in the beaten egg mix. Roll the eggplant strips in the cracker meal. Fill a heavy saucepot with vegetable oil (about 4 inches up from the bottom) and heat it on the stove to 350°F, keeping a thermometer in the oil at all times to prevent overheating and igniting the oil. Fry the eggplant strips for about 4 to 5 minutes. Drain on absorbent paper. Sprinkle with seasoned salt to taste and the grated cheese.

MAKES 4 SERVINGS

Calamari Fritto

(FRIED CALAMARI)

Gaetano Carbone discovered fried calamari at Leon's restaurant in New Haven. In order to get the recipe from Leon's chef, Guy swapped him his own recipe for eggplant. The fried squid was a huge hit with Carbone's customers, as well as among the Carbone family. Instead of offering his boys ice cream cones after baseball games, Guy gave his boys bags of fried calamari, which they adored. It is generally agreed that the calamari at Carbone's is the best in the universe.

4	cups all-purpose flour
½	cup confectioners' sugar
1	teaspoon salt
1	teaspoon pepper
1	pound calamari, cleaned and julienned
1	cup milk
	Vegetable oil
	Seasoned salt

In a bowl combine the flour, sugar, salt, and pepper. Dip the calamari strips in the milk and then separate them on a strainer. Dust the strips with the seasoned flour. Fill a heavy sauce pot with vegetable oil (about 4 inches up from the bottom) and heat it on the stove to 350°F, keeping a thermometer in the oil at all times to prevent overheating and ignition of the oil. Fry the calamari for about 2 to 3 minutes. Drain on absorbent paper. Sprinkle with seasoned salt before serving.

MAKES 4 SERVINGS

Peperoni Imbottiti alla Siciliana

(SICILIAN STUFFED PEPPERS)

Billie Carbone especially likes this traditional Sicilian stuffed pepper recipe because of its liberal inclusion of anchovies. In the Italian kitchen as configured by the Carbone family, anchovies are practically a basic food group.

12	Italian peppers
½	cup olive oil
2	cloves garlic
12	anchovy fillets
2	tablespoons chopped, washed capers
2	tablespoons chopped Italian parsley
½	teaspoon ground black pepper
3	cups breadcrumbs
½	cup grated Parmesan cheese
12	slices tomato

Preheat the oven to 400°F. Wash, dry, and seed the peppers, reserving the caps with stems. In a saucepan heat the oil over medium heat and brown the garlic; discard the garlic. Add the anchovies to the oil and stir until dissolved. Remove the pan from the heat. Add the capers, parsley, and black pepper. Thoroughly mix the breadcrumbs and Parmesan cheese in a bowl and add the anchovy/oil mixture. Spoon the mixture into the peppers loosely, adding alternate slices of tomato. Place the caps on the peppers to hold in the mixture. Put the peppers in a prepared baking pan and cover with a sheet of wax paper. Bake for 20 minutes, or until tender.

MAKES 6 SERVINGS

Formaggio en Carrozza

(CHEESE IN CARRIAGE)

Guy Carbone speculates that this fried-cheese dish was named after the "carousel" of a merry-go-round because the cheese goes around the bread. His version includes prosciutto in the sandwich, making it a variation of a classic Monte Cristo. "I call it Italian grilled cheese with French toast," Guy jokes. While many restaurants serve their version under a mantle of red tomato sauce, here Anchovy and Caper Sauce is the preferred topping.

16	*slices white bread*
32	*slices mozzarella cheese*
16	*slices paper-thin prosciutto*
½	*cup all-purpose flour*
3	*eggs, beaten*
½	*cup virgin olive oil*
	Freshly ground black pepper
	Anchovy and Caper Sauce (see page 68)

Trim the crusts from the slices of bread. Put 4 slices of cheese and 2 slices of prosciutto between each 2 slices of bread. Cut diagonally. Dredge the sandwiches in the flour and dip them into the beaten eggs. Fry in heated, 350-degree oil until golden brown. Serve with freshly ground black pepper and Anchovy and Caper Sauce.

MAKES 4 SERVINGS

Torta di Spinaci Nicola

(SPINACH PIE NICOLA)

Vinnie remembers, "My father's best buddy growing up was Greek, and this was his version of the spanakopita his friend's mother used to make. So we called this Mrs. Nicholas's spinach pie."

1	onion, finely diced
1	tablespoon butter
4	pounds spinach, cooked and drained
¾	cup ricotta cheese
½	cup grated Parmesan cheese
4	eggs, beaten
½	cup diced prosciutto
	Freshly ground black pepper
10	plus 8 slices phyllo (filo) dough

Sauté the onion in butter over medium heat. Mix together the spinach, ricotta cheese, Parmesan cheese, eggs, prosciutto, sautéed onions, and black pepper to taste in a bowl. Preheat the oven to 425°F. Brush a sheet pan with butter and cover with 10 of the phyllo slices. Generously brush the phyllo layer with butter. Pour the spinach/cheese mixture on the phyllo and top that with a layer of 8 phyllo slices. Top with any remaining ricotta. Bake in the oven for 15 minutes.

MAKES 8 TO 10 SERVINGS

Caponatina Siciliana

(SICILIAN RELISH)

Italian ratatouille" is how Vinnie Carbone refers to this zesty eggplant relish. He recommends it as a companion to lamb dishes, or simply used to mix with a pasta of your choice.

2	*eggplants*
	Salt and pepper
1	*whole clove garlic*
½	*plus ½ cup olive oil*
2	*cups diced celery*
¼	*cup diced onion*
2	*cups diced tomatoes*
½	*teaspoon black pepper*
1	*teaspoon dried oregano*
½	*cup washed capers*
6	*tablespoons balsamic or wine vinegar*
½	*cup chopped, pitted Sicilian green olives*
	Salt

Wash and dice the eggplants, leaving the skin on. Place the eggplant in a colander, sprinkle with salt and pepper, and allow to drain for 1 hour. Brown the garlic cloves in a medium skillet in ½ cup of olive oil over medium heat. Discard the garlic and fry all of the eggplant in small amounts and then put it in a large bowl. Sauté the celery slowly until tender. Put it in the bowl with the eggplant. Sauté the onion in the remaining ½ cup olive oil until translucent. Put the onion in the bowl with the eggplant and celery. Drain the oil that has settled in the bottom of the bowl into the frying pan. Add the diced tomatoes to the oil and cook for 30 minutes. Add the tomatoes to the mixture in the bowl. Add the oregano, capers, vinegar, olives, and salt to taste. Toss thoroughly. Refrigerate for at least 2 hours before using.

MAKES 8 SERVINGS

Prosciutto e Melone

(ITALIAN HAM AND MELON)

This is a basic Italian antipasto or snack that balances sweet and salty. As a two-ingredient dish, its deliciousness depends entirely on the ripeness of the cantaloupe or honeydew melon and the quality of the prosciutto, which should be sliced see-through thin.

1	melon
8	very thin slices prosciutto di Parma

Cut the melon in half and remove the seeds. Cut the melon in eight slices and remove the rinds from each slice. Wrap one slice of prosciutto around each slice of melon. Serve chilled.

MAKES 8 SERVINGS

Vongole Casino

(CLAMS CASINO)

When we asked around the Carbone's kitchen to find out where they got clams for their Clams Casino, one wisecracker answered, "From the ocean." In fact, the tender littlenecks that work best come from the cold North Atlantic waters off Rhode Island and Massachusetts.

16	*clams*
	Rock salt or washed pebbles
¼	*cup chopped green peppers*
¼	*cup chopped onions*
2	*tablespoons butter*
½	*pimiento, chopped*
1	*tablespoon chopped parsley*
	Juice of ½ lemon
	Pinch of paprika
	Dash of Worcestershire sauce
	Salt and pepper
2	*slices bacon*

Preheat the oven to 450°F. Wash and open the clams. Place the shucked clams on a half shell on a bed of rock salt or washed pebbles. Sauté the peppers and onions in the butter for 5 to 8 minutes. Add the pimiento, parsley, lemon juice, paprika, Worcestershire sauce, and salt and pepper to taste. Place 1 tablespoon of the mixture on each open clam. Cut each slice of bacon into eight pieces and place one piece on each clam. Bake in the oven for 5 minutes.

MAKES 4 SERVINGS

Vongole all'Origano

(BAKED STUFFED CLAMS)

Here's an oceanic appetizer that is similar to Clams Casino, but made without the bacon. Use freshly grated Parmesan to give it a flavorful snap.

16	clams
	Rock salt or washed pebbles
¼	cup olive oil
1	whole clove garlic
1	cup breadcrumbs
¼	cup grated Parmesan cheese
1	tablespoon dried oregano
	Freshly ground black pepper
2	tablespoons melted butter
16	lemon wedges

Preheat the oven to 450°F. Wash and open the clams. Place the shucked clams on a half shell on a bed of rock salt or washed pebbles. Heat the oil, brown the garlic, and discard the garlic. Place the breadcrumbs in a bowl with the cheese, oregano, and pepper to taste; mix with the garlic oil. Sprinkle the mixture on each clam. Drizzle butter on each clam and bake in the oven for 5 minutes. Serve with lemon wedges.

MAKES 4 SERVINGS

Cozza Posilipo

(MUSSELS IN TOMATO SAUCE)

Posillipo generally refers to the process of steaming shellfish in its own broth. Guy reminisced about the early days of the restaurant when mussels cost a mere $3 per bushel. "Everybody thought they were poison!" he says. "You couldn't give them away. We were the first to serve mussels around here; nobody else would touch them fifty years ago."

1	whole clove garlic
4	tablespoons olive oil
2	tablespoons butter
2	tablespoons chopped onion
1	tablespoon chopped celery
1	tablespoon chopped fennel
2	tablespoons chopped carrots
3	leaves fresh basil
2	tablespoons sherry
2	cups peeled canned tomatoes, hand crushed
40	mussels
2	tablespoons fresh parsley
	Salt and pepper

Brown the garlic in the oil and butter in a skillet over medium heat. Add the onion, celery, fennel, carrots, and basil. Cook for 5 minutes. Add the sherry and tomatoes and cook for 30 minutes. Remove from the heat and put in a blender or pass through a sieve. Wash the mussels and put them in a pot; then add the sauce and return to the heat. Cover and cook for 8 minutes. Add the parsley and salt and pepper to taste; stir and cook for 2 minutes more.

MAKES 4 SERVINGS

Cremini Imbottiti

(STUFFED MUSHROOMS)

Mushrooms are plentiful throughout much of Italy and they are used in recipes from many regions. "When I started in the kitchen, we could get only two kinds of mushrooms," Guy Carbone says. "I'd call our supplier and say I need large or small. Today, there are so many more choices."

20	*large cremini mushrooms*
1	*clove garlic, minced*
1¼	*cups virgin olive oil*
½	*cup chopped mushroom stems*
¼	*cup diced onion*
1	*cup breadcrumbs*
¼	*cup grated Parmesan cheese*
½	*teaspoon chopped fresh thyme*
2	*tablespoons black pepper*
2	*tablespoons melted butter*
1	*teaspoon chopped fresh sage*
½	*cup chopped walnuts*

Preheat the oven to 400°F. Wash the mushrooms, remove the stems, and dry the caps. Sauté the garlic in the olive oil; discard the garlic when brown. Add the chopped mushroom stems and diced onion; sauté for 10 minutes. Add the breadcrumbs, cheese, thyme, pepper, butter, sage, and walnuts and mix thoroughly. Stuff the mushroom caps, place them on an oiled baking pan, and bake them in the oven for 10 minutes.

MAKES 4 SERVINGS

Aglio Arrostito

(Roasted Garlic)

It is possible to roast garlic and offer whole cloves of it to spread on bread. At Carbone's roasted garlic is made a gallon at a time for use in other recipes.

Whole garlic cloves
Olive oil (blended with vegetable oil)*

Method 1: Stovetop

Place the whole peeled garlic in a sauté pan over medium heat and cover with the olive oil. (You can use the expensive oils if you prefer but you're going to infuse the garlic flavor and lose the olive flavor when you do this procedure.) Cook slowly until the garlic just begins to turn golden brown and then take the pan off the heat because the oil is going to remain at the cooking point for a little longer. Let the garlic and oil cool before straining. You can use the garlic immediately or refrigerate it in the oil for up to a week.

Method 2: Oven

Preheat the oven to 350°F. Place the whole peeled garlic in a roasting pan and cover it with olive oil. Cover the pan with aluminum foil and cook it in the oven for about 30 minutes. (All ovens are different so cooking times will vary.) It is better to err on the side of undercooking because the oil is going to remain at the cooking point for a little longer. Let the garlic and oil cool before straining. You can use the garlic immediately or refrigerate it in the oil for up to a week.

*Note: Olive oil has a lower burning point than vegetable oil. If you can't find the blended oil (10 percent olive, 90 percent vegetable) then just use 100 percent vegetable oil.

· STONE PIES ·

(Torta di Pietra)

Margherita Stone Pie
Spinach, Potato, and Roasted Garlic Stone Pie
Clam and Pancetta Stone Pie
Grilled Pear with Stilton Cheese and Foie Gras
Prosciutto with Anchovy and Gorgonzola Cheese
LaCava Stone Pie
Pesto Stone Pie

Torta di Pietra alla Pomodoro

(MARGHERITA STONE PIE)

Vinnie Carbone's eyes light up when he talks about his restaurant's stone pies. Only two are listed on the everyday menu—a classic Margherita (tomato, mozzarella, and pesto) and a Fico di Parma (grilled figs and prosciutto). But almost every day, every meal, other pies are made depending on what interesting ingredients are on hand and the imagination of the cooks. What they all have in common is a thin crust that is first "marked" and flavored on the grill, then cooked on a pizza stone until done. To make this style of pizza you will need a pizza stone.

4	ounces pizza dough (store bought or homemade)*
1	ounce extra virgin olive oil
1	to 2 cloves garlic, chopped
1½	cups chopped, canned Roma tomatoes
3	tablespoons chopped fresh basil
	Fresh ground black pepper
1	cup sliced fresh mozzarella
½	cup grated Romano cheese

Preheat the grill on high (the hotter the better). With a rolling pin and a liberal amount of all-purpose flour, roll out the dough to the size of your baking stone. (Uniformly round is nice but a shell of even thickness is more important.) Shake off any excess flour and place the shell on the hot grill. Cook 2 to 3 minutes per side.

Preheat the oven and the pizza stone to 400°F. With a spoon or your hand, spread the oil and garlic evenly on the pizza shell and spread on the tomatoes, basil, and black pepper to taste. Sprinkle the mozzarella and Romano cheeses on top. Slide the pie onto the preheated stone and bake 8 to 10 minutes, or until evenly brown, all the toppings are cooked through, and the cheeses are melted.

MAKES 1 TO 2 SERVINGS

*Note: Use approximately 4 ounces (about the size of a small fist) of dough for a 10-inch pizza. Use 3 ounces of dough for an 8-inch pizza.

Variation: Use 1 ripe native tomato, sliced, in place of the canned Roma tomatoes.

51

PIZZA, PLAIN AND FANCY

Twenty years ago pizza would not have been mentioned in a Carbone's cookbook. Pizza griglia, baked on the porous stone floor of a hearth, is a recent addition to the menu.

It wasn't until the 1970s that Americans began thinking about pizza as a dish that could be deluxe. To most of us, pizza was nothing more than an inexpensive snack food, originally found in Italian neighborhoods, then popularized by companies such as Domino's and Pizza Hut. Pizza was always topped with tomato sauce and plenty of bland mozzarella cheese, plus maybe sausage or pepperoni. But as Italian food has been rediscovered and redefined, pizza itself has expanded beyond such fundamentals. It is still the nation's favorite cheap-eats take-out meal, but pizza also provides an opportunity for creative chefs to apply their talents.

Carbone's menu lists only two kinds of pizza: fico di parma (a fabulously luxurious combination of grilled figs and prosciutto) and margherita, which is the kitchen's version of what was arguably the world's first pizza, created in the late 1800s by a Neapolitan baker named Raffaele Esposito. The legend is that Esposito wanted to make a special dish for King Umberto and Queen Margherita when they came to visit, so he topped a flatbread with red tomatoes, white mozzarella cheese, and green basil—the colors of Italy. The dish caught on and pizza was born. Carbone's Margherita pizza is Esposito's idea, but topped with garlic-rich pesto rather than basic basil leaves.

As is typical of Carbone's, many of the kitchen's best pizzas are not printed on the menu. Any customer with a passion for pizza should inquire what kind of stone pies the chefs can prepare that day. Vinnie Carbone said that he and Michael love experimenting with pizza toppings, based on whatever interesting ingredients are at hand. Among their more fantastic creations have been a shrimp curry pizza with cumin and a little mascarpone cheese "to smooth it out," and the most outrageous one of all is a pizza topped with foie gras, warm enough to be on the verge of melting, and sweet marinated grilled peaches. Don't try asking Domino's to deliver one of those!

Torta di Pietra con Spinaci, Patata e Aglio Arrostito

(SPINACH, POTATO, AND ROASTED GARLIC STONE PIE)

This was chef Mike McDowell's creation for making a stone pie that is the flatbread version of the "spinach bread" so popular in Italian bakeries of the Northeast.

4	ounces pizza dough (store bought or homemade)*
½	cup roasted garlic (see page 48)
1	tablespoon oil (from roasting the garlic)
2	to 3 ounces fresh spinach, stemmed
½	cup potato, baked, roasted, or mashed (from leftovers)
1	cup shredded Asiago cheese
	Salt and pepper
1	cup chopped native tomatoes (optional)

Preheat the grill on high (the hotter the better). With a rolling pin and a liberal amount of all-purpose flour, roll out the dough to the size of your baking stone. (Uniformly round is nice but a shell of even thickness is more important.) Shake off any excess flour and place the shell on the hot grill. Cook 2 to 3 minutes per side.

Preheat the oven and the pizza stone to 400°F. With a spoon or your hand, rub the garlic and oil into the grilled shell. Spread the spinach evenly over the shell and top with the potato and shredded cheese. Salt and pepper to taste. Add chopped native tomatoes when you can get them for a variation. Slide the pie onto the preheated stone and bake 8 to 10 minutes, or until evenly brown and all the toppings are cooked through and the cheeses are melted.

MAKES 1 TO 2 SERVINGS

*Note: Use approximately 4 ounces (about the size of a small fist) of dough for a 10-inch pizza. Use 3 ounces of dough for an 8-inch pizza.

Torta di Pietra Vongola e Pancetta Affumicata

(CLAM AND PANCETTA STONE PIE)

Pepe's Pizzeria Napoletana of New Haven has built a national reputation for its white clam pizza—a pie topped with clams, oil, and seasonings but no red sauce or mozzarella cheese. This is chef Paul Rafala's version of the New Haven signature dish.

4	ounces pizza dough (store bought or homemade)*
1	to 2 cloves garlic, chopped
1	tablespoon extra virgin olive oil
½	cup chopped clams (freshly shucked or canned)
¼	to ½ cup pancetta (bacon), diced, blanched, and drained
1	ounce fresh basil, chopped
¼	to ½ cup grated Romano cheese

Preheat the grill on high (the hotter the better). With a rolling pin and a liberal amount of all-purpose flour, roll out the dough to the size of your baking stone. (Uniformly round is nice but a shell of even thickness is more important.) Shake off any excess flour and place the shell on the hot grill. Cook 2 to 3 minutes per side.

Preheat the oven and the pizza stone to 400°F. Mix the garlic and olive oil and spread evenly over the shell. Spread the clams, bacon, and basil over the top. Top with the Romano cheese. Slide the pie onto the preheated stone and bake 8 to 10 minutes, or until evenly brown and all the toppings are cooked through and the cheeses are melted.

MAKES 1 TO 2 SERVINGS

*Note: Use approximately 4 ounces (about the size of a small fist) of dough for a 10-inch pizza. Use 3 ounces of dough for an 8-inch pizza.

Pera alla Griglia con Formaggio di Stilton e Foie Gras

(GRILLED PEAR WITH STILTON CHEESE AND FOIE GRAS)

One of the catering jobs Carbone's does annually is a holiday party for customer Ted Rossi. A few years ago Vinnie & Co. created this ultraluxurious stone pie for Mr. Rossi's celebration meal.

4	ounces pizza dough (store bought or homemade)*
1	tablespoon extra virgin olive oil
¼	cup chopped roasted garlic
1	fresh pear, marinated several hours in port wine, sliced, and grilled
½	cup crumbled Stilton cheese
3	to 4 ounces prepared foie gras, thinly sliced

Preheat the grill on high (the hotter the better). With a rolling pin and a liberal amount of all-purpose flour, roll out the dough to the size of your baking stone. (Uniformly round is nice but a shell of even thickness is more important.) Shake off any excess flour and place the shell on the hot grill. Cook 2 to 3 minutes per side.

Preheat the oven and pizza stone to 400°F. Rub the shell with the olive oil and roasted garlic. Place the grilled pear slices flat to cover the shell. Top with the Stilton cheese. Slide the pie onto the preheated stone and bake until the cheese is three-quarters of the way melted, about 5 minutes. Remove the pizza and top it with the foie gras slices. Return it to the oven for thirty seconds or so just to melt the foie gras slightly.

MAKES 1 TO 2 SERVINGS

*Note: Use approximately 4 ounces (about the size of a small fist) of dough for a 10-inch pizza. Use 3 ounces of dough for an 8-inch pizza.

Note: Sliced, fresh, black mission figs make a good substitute for the pears; also, a little drizzle of truffle oil at the end is nice.

Prosciutto con Acciuga e Gorgonzola

(PROSCIUTTO WITH ANCHOVY AND GORGONZOLA CHEESE)

Carbone's recommends serving the prosciutto and gorgonzola cheese pizza with a dry white wine.

4	ounces pizza dough (store bought or homemade)*
¼	cup chopped garlic
1	teaspoon olive oil
3	to 4 anchovy fillets, chopped
1	to 2 ounces prosciutto, very thinly sliced
½	cup Gorgonzola cheese
	Freshly cracked black or red pepper

Preheat the grill on high (the hotter the better). With a rolling pin and a liberal amount of all-purpose flour, roll out the dough to the size of your baking stone. (Uniformly round is nice but a shell of even thickness is more important.) Shake off any excess flour and place the shell on the hot grill. Cook 2 to 3 minutes per side.

Preheat the oven and pizza stone to 400°F. Mix together the garlic, oil, and anchovies and spread evenly on the shell. Layer the prosciutto to cover the pie. Sprinkle the top with the Gorgonzola cheese and pepper to taste. Slide the pie onto the preheated stone and bake 8 to 10 minutes, or until evenly brown and all the toppings are cooked through and the cheeses are melted.

MAKES 1 TO 2 SERVINGS

*Note: Use approximately 4 ounces (about the size of a small fist) of dough for a 10-inch pizza. Use 3 ounces of dough for an 8-inch pizza.

Variation: Substitute thinly sliced Genoa salami for the prosciutto.

Torta di Pietra alla La Cava

(LaCava Stone Pie)

Because of the popularity of Chicken LaCava, Carbone's decided to put the same ingredients on top of a stone pie that has become a great hit with customers.

4	ounces pizza dough (store bought or homemade)*
¼	cup chopped roasted garlic
½	cup crumbled cooked Italian sausage
½	cup diced chicken (grilled is best)
½	cup chopped sweet roasted peppers (canned or fresh)
½	cup sliced pickled hot cherry peppers (stuffed, if you can get them)
½	cup shredded Asiago cheese

Preheat the grill on high (the hotter the better). With a rolling pin and a liberal amount of all-purpose flour, roll out the dough to the size of your baking stone. (Uniformly round is nice but a shell of even thickness is more important.) Shake off any excess flour and place the shell on the hot grill. Cook 2 to 3 minutes per side.

Preheat the oven and the pizza stone to 400°F. Rub the garlic onto the shell and spread the sausage and chicken all around. Add the sweet peppers and hot cherry peppers (allow a little juice to flavor the pie) and top with the cheese. Slide the pie onto the preheated stone and bake 8 to 10 minutes, or until evenly brown and the cheese is melted.

MAKES 1 TO 2 SERVINGS

*Note: Use approximately 4 ounces (about the size of a small fist) of dough for a 10-inch pizza. Use 3 ounces of dough for an 8-inch pizza.

Torta di Pietra alla Pesto

(PESTO STONE PIE)

This is a pie you want to make when you get a bunch of garden-fresh basil and parsley to go with it. While it is possible to add sun dried tomatoes or hot chili peppers for color and zest, we like the rich green flavor of this pie without the extra jolt.

4	ounces pizza dough (store bought or homemade)*		1	bunch freshly picked parsley (about ½ cup)
¼	plus ¼ cup best quality extra virgin olive oil		1	pinch kosher salt
				Freshly ground black pepper
2	to 3 cloves garlic		½	cup or more grated Romano cheese
1	to 2 ounces pine nuts or walnuts, slightly browned			
				Shredded Asiago cheese
1	bunch freshly picked basil, stemmed (about 1 cup)			

Preheat the grill on high (the hotter the better). With a rolling pin and a liberal amount of all-purpose flour, roll out the dough to the size of your baking stone. (Uniformly round is nice but a shell of even thickness is more important.) Shake off any excess flour and place the shell on the hot grill. Cook 2 to 3 minutes per side.

Preheat the oven and pizza stone to 400°F. In a food processor (must have a sharp blade), combine ¼ cup olive oil with the garlic and pine nuts; grind to a paste. Add the basil, parsley, salt, and pepper to taste. Grind the mixture to a paste, adding the remaining olive oil. Add the Romano cheese and grind again until the pesto is smooth. Spread the pesto on the prepared shell and top the pie with shredded Asiago cheese. Slide the pie onto the preheated stone and bake 8 to 10 minutes, or until evenly brown and the cheese is melted.

MAKES 1 TO 2 SERVINGS

*Note: Use approximately 4 ounces (about the size of a small fist) of dough for a 10-inch pizza. Use 3 ounces of dough for an 8-inch pizza.

Variation: Sauté approximately 1 to 2 cups sliced fresh mushrooms with the Romano cheese. Add a little soy sauce for a variation on the basil flavor.

LOVE AT CARBONE'S

Ann-Marie Brodeur, a longtime member of the Carbone's waitstaff, offered these words of appreciation for what working at the restaurant has meant to her: "Not only have some people found satisfying careers at Carbone's, but some have actually found lifetime happiness. One such example would be our bar manager and myself."

Although Ann-Marie isn't quite sure how they got together in the first place, she remembers greeting Bob every morning with a hearty hello. And for three years, she received nothing more than a grunt in response. After time, another employee informed her of Bob's strong attraction to her. She was certain they would not hit it off, but agreed to go out with him just to prove it. Well, she was wrong. They were married a year later, have two children, and have been happy for fourteen years.

Bob holds court every day at the Carbone's bar. You would likely meet Ann-Marie in the dining room as she flames a spinach salad or liqueur-spiked after-dinner coffee.

Bar Manager Bob Brodeur and his wife, Carbone's sales assistant, Ann-Marie.

· SAUCES ·

(Salse)

Naples-Style Tomato Sauce
Seaman's Sauce
Cream Sauce
Mornay Sauce
Simple Tomato Sauce
Meat Sauce from Bologna
Anchovy and Caper Sauce
Leon's Sauce
Green Sauce
Mushroom Wine Sauce
Scampi Romance Sauce
Gorgonzola Sauce

Salsa di Pomodora alla Napoletana

(NAPLES-STYLE TOMATO SAUCE)

Tomatoes are popular throughout Italy, but their use in cooking has long been most closely associated with Naples. This particular red tomato sauce is sweetened with carrots and enriched with wine.

¼	cup olive oil
1	clove garlic
¼	cup diced onion
3	tablespoons diced carrot
1	tablespoon chopped Italian parsley
2	tablespoons chopped celery
¼	cup red wine
2½	pounds tomatoes
2	basil leaves
	Salt and pepper

Heat the oil in a saucepan over medium heat and brown the garlic; discard the garlic. Add the onions, carrots, parsley, and celery. Sauté for 5 minutes. Add the wine and cook for 2 minutes longer. Add the tomatoes and cook for 30 minutes. Add the basil, and salt and pepper to taste. Cook for 10 minutes longer. Pass through a sieve or purée in a blender.

MAKES 1 QUART

Salsa alla Marinara

(SEAMAN'S SAUCE)

When Charlie Carbone made Seaman's Sauce, he always incorporated anchovies. He tossed the sauce with pasta and also used it in many of his shellfish recipes.

¼	cup olive oil	¼	teaspoon oregano
2	cloves garlic	1	tablespoon chopped parsley
4	tablespoons onion	4	tablespoons chopped anchovies (optional)
2½	pounds tomatoes		Salt and pepper

Heat the oil in a saucepan over medium heat, brown the garlic, and discard the garlic. Sauté the onion for 5 minutes, and then add the tomatoes. Cook for 30 minutes. Add the oregano, chopped parsley, anchovies, and salt and pepper to taste. Cook for 10 minutes longer. Pass through a sieve or purée in a blender.

MAKES 1 QUART

Salsa di Crema

(CREAM SAUCE)

A good roux, such as this, is the foundation for many sauces. It can also be used to thicken soups or stews. When you make it, the color will gradually darken from cream white to honey yellow. Whichever way you like it, the salsa must be tended on the stove constantly. Any roux, once burned, is ruined.

2	tablespoons flour
4	tablespoons melted butter
4	cups milk

For a thin sauce blend the flour and melted butter and cook over low heat for 2 minutes. Stirring constantly, gradually add the milk. Bring to a boil and simmer gently until thickened.

To make a thick sauce, use ¼ cup butter and ¼ cup flour, and then follow the directions above.

MAKES 1 QUART

Salsa Mornay al Formaggio
(MORNAY SAUCE)

A Mornay sauce is a classic béchamel with shredded cheese added for flavor and richness. French Mornay includes Gruyere and/or Parmesan. This version of Carbone's isn't French and isn't really Italian. It is more evocative of the Italian-American kitchen, using Cheddar cheese rather than a more typical old-country one.

2	tablespoons flour
4	tablespoons melted butter
4	cups milk
1	teaspoon dry mustard
1	teaspoon white peppercorns
¼	teaspoon Worcestershire sauce
½	pound Cheddar cheese, grated or chopped

Blend the flour and melted butter and cook over low heat for 2 minutes. Stirring constantly, gradually add the milk. Add the dry mustard, peppercorns, and Worcestershire sauce before bringing to boil. Bring to a boil and gradually add the cheese, stirring constantly. Let simmer gently until thickened.

MAKES 1 QUART

Salsa Semplice

(SIMPLE TOMATO SAUCE)

For every Italian, there is a recipe for tomato sauce," Vinnie says. This is a simple one that can be seasoned and spiced up or down to taste.

¼	cup olive oil
2	cloves garlic
2½	pounds tomatoes
4	fresh basil leaves
	Freshly ground black pepper
	Salt

In a saucepan heat the oil over medium heat, brown the garlic, and discard the garlic. Add the tomatoes and cook for 30 minutes. Add the fresh basil and the salt and pepper to taste. Pass through a sieve or purée in a blender.

MAKES 1 QUART

Ragu alla Bolognese
(MEAT SAUCE FROM BOLOGNA)

The old people threw nothing away," Guy reminds us. "Whatever bits and pieces of meat they had on hand—beef, ham—went into the Bolognese."

3	tablespoons olive oil
3	tablespoons butter
3	tablespoons diced onion
3	tablespoons diced carrot
3	tablespoons diced celery
1½	pounds crushed tomatoes
2	cups ground beef
1	cup chopped pork
1	cup chopped veal
¼	cup dry wine
¾	cup light cream
¼	teaspoon nutmeg
	Salt and pepper

Mix the olive oil and butter and heat in a skillet over medium heat. Sauté the onion, carrot, and celery for 5 minutes. Add the tomatoes and cook for 20 minutes on medium-low. Put through a sieve or purée in a blender and transfer to a cooking pot. Sauté the beef, pork, and veal in the remaining oil and the wine for 5 minutes. Add the tomatoes and vegetables and cook for another 10 minutes. Add the cream, nutmeg, and salt and pepper to taste. Bring to a boil and simmer gently for another 5 minutes.

MAKES 2 QUARTS

*Note: This is good served over egg noodles.

Carbone's Cookbook

Salsa di Acciughe e Capperi

(ANCHOVY AND CAPER SAUCE)

This vivid all-purpose sauce is used to accent dishes from Formaggio en Carrozza (see page 40) to spaghetti noodles. It has been a Carbone favorite for generations. Vinnie remembers bowls of it being on the kitchen table to be used as a dip for fennel or celery.

¼	cup olive oil
2	cloves garlic
4	anchovy fillets
24	capers, washed and chopped
1	tablespoon vinegar or juice of 1 lemon
1	tablespoon chopped fresh parsley
2	ounces (½ stick) butter

Heat the oil in a saucepan over medium heat, brown the garlic, and discard the garlic. Add the anchovies until dissolved and stir. Add the vinegar/lemon and capers. Stir in the butter and parsley and remove from the heat.

MAKES 1 CUP (ABOUT 4 SERVINGS)

OIL AND VINEGAR

For many years, cruets of vinegar and oil were as emblematic of an Italian restaurant as a wicker-clad Chianti bottle. Generally the vinegar was red wine vinegar, and the oil was *olio d'oliva*, an acidic emulsion made from what was left when olives were pressed to make "virgin" oils. Oil and vinegar enlivened by garlic and spices are the pillars of traditional Italian salad dressing, and they remain basic ingredients in the Italian kitchen today.

Both oil and vinegar have gone uptown. Beginning in the late 1970s, the culinary world discovered the joy of good olive oil, once rarely known outside of Mediterranean kitchens. And vinegar, which most American cooks knew as either red (wine) or white (cider) blossomed into a multipurpose condiment found in dishes from salads to desserts and even, in its most refined incarnations, drizzled over ice and sipped like sweet/tart *eau de vie*. *Balsamico*, named for its balsam scent, has been a player in the world of food fashion for a couple of decades now. The best of it, known as *extra vecchia*, takes at least twenty-five years to produce, and the best of that—which is the stuff people sip by the droplet—is aged in wood barrels for over a century.

According to the *Denominazione d'Origine Controllata,* a kind of Italian FDA, grades of olive oil are:

- *Olio de sansa d'oliva*: made from the dregs of pressed olives
- *Olivo d'oliva*: a blend of oils, including olive, over 4% acidity
- *Vergine*: no more than 4% acidity
- *Fino vergine*: no more than 3% acidity
- *Sopprafino vergine*: no more than 1.5% acidity
- *Extra vergine*: less than 1% acidity, made from the first pressing of the olives

Salsa Leone

(LEON'S SAUCE)

Salsa Leone was a late-summer special nearly every day of the week back when tomatoes grew in everybody's garden around Franklin Avenue. "We were overloaded with tomatoes," Guy remembers. "So many people brought them here by the bushel." Salsa Leone, which puts them to good use, was named for Leon's restaurant in New Haven, another of the Northeast's landmark Italian kitchens. Charlie Carbone used to swap recipes with Leon's; for this one, he exchanged his recipe for eggplant, but the artichoke hearts were his addition.

½	*cup olive oil*
1	*clove garlic, finely minced*
½	*cup diced onions*
6	*ounces sausage meat*
3	*ounces ground prosciutto*
2	*tablespoons sherry wine*
1½	*pounds plum tomatoes, chopped*
4	*leaves fresh basil*
4	*hearts of artichokes, cut in half*

Heat the oil in a saucepan over medium heat and sauté the garlic and onions. Add the sausage, prosciutto, and wine and simmer for 5 minutes. Add the tomatoes and cook for 20 minutes. Add the basil and artichoke hearts and simmer slowly for 5 minutes longer. Serve on cooked pasta.

MAKES 6 TO 8 SERVINGS

Pesto alla Genovese

(Green Sauce)

My father used to make his pesto with salted peanuts," Guy Carbone laughs. "He loved Planter's because they added a salty kick to the recipe." Nowadays, Carbone's does not use peanuts in its pesto, but Vinnie Carbone does admit that once you've had it made with them, its flavor is one your taste buds will not want to forget.

1	cup chopped fresh basil leaves
¼	cup chopped fresh parsley
4	cloves garlic
½	cup grated Parmesan cheese
¼	teaspoon cracked black pepper
1	cup olive oil
¼	cup butter
¼	cup pine nuts and walnuts

Place basil, parsley, garlic, Parmesan, pepper, olive oil, butter, and walnuts in the work bowl of a food processor. Process until a smooth paste. (You may need to do this in small quantities.) Heat in a saucepan over medium heat for 10 minutes.

MAKES 6 SERVINGS

Salsa di Funghi al Vino

(MUSHROOM WINE SAUCE)

This is a great sauce for beef or venison; we also like it drizzled onto a good Parmesan risotto.

8	ounces mushrooms (use a variety for best results)
2	ounces virgin olive oil
¼	cup Marsala wine
¼	cup (½ stick) butter
	Pinch of roux*
	Salt and pepper

Sauté the mushrooms in the olive oil over medium-high heat until tender. Add the wine and reduce by simmering for 2 to 3 minutes. Add the butter with the roux and stir until melted. Add the salt and pepper to taste.

MAKES 4 SERVINGS

*Note: Make the roux by melting 1 teaspoon of butter in a small saucepan and mixing in 1 teaspoon of flour until combined.

Salsa di Scampi alla Romantica

(SCAMPI ROMANCE SAUCE)

Creamy and vivid with spice and horseradish, this sauce transforms gentle-natured shrimp into a dish that sparkles with soulfulness.

4	*ounces heavy cream*
¼	*cup (½ stick) butter*
1	*teaspoon Dijon mustard*
1	*teaspoon Worcestershire sauce*
3	*dashes Tabasco*
2	*ounces capers*
1	*teaspoon prepared horseradish*
1	*tablespoon grated Romano cheese*
¼	*teaspoon black pepper*
1	*teaspoon freshly chopped parsley*
8	*jumbo shrimp, cooked*

Reduce the cream and butter by simmering for 2 to 3 minutes in a saucepan over medium-high heat. Add the mustard, Worcestershire sauce, Tabasco, capers, horseradish, cheese, black pepper, and parsley and stir well. Cook for 2 more minutes. Pour the sauce over the shrimp and serve.

MAKES 4 SERVINGS

Salsa di Gorgonzola

(GORGONZOLA SAUCE)

Make this mighty, zesty sauce when you have good Gorgonzola cheese and use it on your favorite pasta. Because it keeps well in the refrigerator, it's great to keep on hand for those meals when all you want to do is cook pasta. If using refrigerated sauce, warm it up before mixing with the noodles of your choice.

¼	cup virgin olive oil
2	anchovy fillets
1	teaspoon chopped fresh garlic
6	ounces Gorgonzola cheese
¼	cup (½ stick) butter
⅛	teaspoon black pepper
¼	teaspoon chopped fresh rosemary
1	teaspoon chopped fresh parsley

In a small saucepan heat the oil and anchovies over medium heat until dissolved. Add the garlic and stir for 1 minute. Lower heat. Add the cheese, butter, pepper, rosemary, and parsley and stir together until a smooth sauce develops. Hold at room temperature for use. This sauce refrigerates well.

MAKES ABOUT 1½ CUPS

· PASTA ·

(Pasta)

Gaetano's Green and White Noodles Bue Bella
Angel Hair Pasta
Shrimp in a Roasted Pepper Sauce over Capellini
Duck Orzo
Risotto "Paella Style"
Lobster and Asparagus Risotto
Ravioli with Ricotta
Baked Eggplant and Macaroni
Linguine and Clam Sauce
Pasta Marzi
Green Noodles with Hog Jowls
Fettuccini Alfredo
Roman-Style Spaghetti
Francesco's Pasta
Pasta Panatula
Basic Pasta Dough
Gaetano's Cannelloni Piedmontese
Gaetano's Cannelloni Neapolitan

Pasta Gaetano alla Bue Bella

(Gaetano's Green and White Noodles Bue Bella)

No one currently at Carbone's could explain exactly what the "Bue Bella" in this recipe means; but all say it has been on the menu since Charlie's time. Guy deduced that it has something to do with "beautiful cheese," referring to the Gorgonzola. With anchovies and butter, it is a powerful sauce, served as a condiment for steaks as well as on pasta.

1	clove garlic, minced
¼	cup (½ stick) butter, melted
1½	ounces (about ¼ cup) Gorgonzola cheese
2	anchovies, minced
⅔	teaspoon chopped parsley
12	ounces green noodles
12	ounces white noodles
½	cup chicken stock (see page 13)
2	to 3 tablespoons Italian sharp cheese (Asiago)
2	to 3 tablespoons Romano cheese
2	teaspoons minced onion
2	teaspoons prosciutto, finely chopped
2	teaspoons olive oil
½	cup cooked fresh green peas

Heat and brown the garlic in the melted butter over medium heat; add the Gorgonzola cheese, anchovies, and parsley. Cook and drain the noodles. Toss with the chicken stock, Italian sharp cheese, and Romano cheese. Add to the cheese sauce. In a separate pan sauté the onion and prosciutto in olive oil over medium heat. Add the peas, and cook for a few minutes. Complete the dish by topping the noodles with the onion mixture.

MAKES 6 SERVINGS

PASTA PRIMER

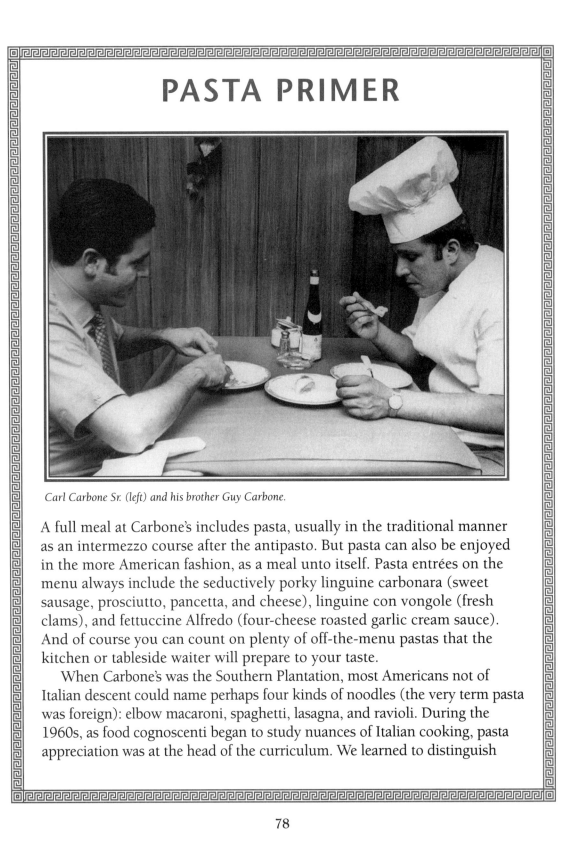

Carl Carbone Sr. (left) and his brother Guy Carbone.

A full meal at Carbone's includes pasta, usually in the traditional manner as an intermezzo course after the antipasto. But pasta can also be enjoyed in the more American fashion, as a meal unto itself. Pasta entrées on the menu always include the seductively porky linguine carbonara (sweet sausage, prosciutto, pancetta, and cheese), linguine con vongole (fresh clams), and fettuccine Alfredo (four-cheese roasted garlic cream sauce). And of course you can count on plenty of off-the-menu pastas that the kitchen or tableside waiter will prepare to your taste.

When Carbone's was the Southern Plantation, most Americans not of Italian descent could name perhaps four kinds of noodles (the very term pasta was foreign): elbow macaroni, spaghetti, lasagna, and ravioli. During the 1960s, as food cognoscenti began to study nuances of Italian cooking, pasta appreciation was at the head of the curriculum. We learned to distinguish pasta di semola di grano duro, made from durum wheat, from pasta all'uovo, which includes eggs, and we discovered that good pasta was at its best prepared al dente ("to the tooth," meaning still slightly chewy). Dozens of unfamiliar noodles appeared on plates, from classical tubes of penne (literally "quill") to such whimsical shapes as ruote ("wagon wheels").

Some appealing pasta shapes, and their literal meanings or brief descriptions:

- **agnolotti**: "priest's caps"
- **capellini**: "angel hair"
- **cappelletti**: stuffed "hats"
- **cavatelli**: small crinkle-edged shells that look like mini folded-over tacos
- **creste di galli**: "cockscomb," looking like a rooster's topknot
- **farfalle**: little "bow ties"
- **fettuccine**: "ribbons"
- **fusilli**: "corkscrews"
- **gemelli**: "twins"; refers to a pair of short noodles twisted together in a spiral
- **gnocchi**: "dumplings"
- **linguine**: "little tongues"
- **manicotti**: long, wide tubes, smooth or ridged. Manicotti means "muffs."
- **orecchiette**: "little ears"
- **pastina**: "tiny dough," referring to itty-bitty pasta shapes often used in soup
- **rigatoni**: short, straight tubes like penne but wider and usually grooved
- **rotini**: springlike spirals
- **spaghettini**: spaghetti, but thinner
- **vermicelli**: "little worms"; very thin strands

Capelli d' Angelo
(ANGEL HAIR PASTA)

The Carbones describe the sauce used in this angelic dish as a delicate version of puttanesca. The recipe has been a kitchen standard for many years, and was once featured in *Bon Appetit* magazine.

2	tablespoons olive oil
¼	cup finely chopped onion
2	cloves garlic, minced
3	anchovy fillets
1	tablespoon chopped Italian parsley
12	Sicilian green olives, chopped and pitted
1	teaspoon capers, washed
½	cup chicken stock (see page 13)
	Milled black pepper
4	cups marinara sauce
	Dash of sherry wine
1½	pounds angel hair pasta, cooked and drained
2	tablespoons butter
	Grated dry ricotta cheese

In a saucepan over medium heat cook the oil, onion, garlic, and anchovies for 3 to 5 minutes (do not turn). Add the parsley, olives, and capers and simmer. Add the chicken stock and pepper to taste and simmer. Add the marinara sauce and sherry wine and simmer gently for 10 more minutes. Toss the pasta gently with the butter. Top with the sauce and grated cheese.

MAKES 6 SERVINGS

Gamberetti en Salsa di Peperoni con Capellini

(SHRIMP IN A ROASTED PEPPER SAUCE OVER CAPELLINI)

What follows is a basic recipe for shrimp to which Carbone's chefs add all kinds of different ingredients to vary the taste of the sauce. Hot pepper flakes or fresh hot peppers go very well, as do different kinds of shellfish or even cooked chicken. It can also be served over grilled salmon and garnished with colorful seasonal sweet peppers.

SAUCE:

3	to 4 seeded red bell peppers
1	large carrot, peeled and roughly chopped
1	large Spanish onion, peeled and roughly chopped
3	to 4 shallots, peeled
3	to 4 fresh oregano sprigs, stemmed
½	plus ¼ cup extra virgin olive oil

	Salt and pepper
1	cup sherry
1½	cups chicken stock (or beef or vegetable)
6	extra large shrimp, peeled and deveined
½	cup mascarpone cheese
	Cooked pasta
1	tablespoon chopped fresh basil

Preheat the oven to 375°F. In a roasting pan place the peppers, carrot, onion, shallots, and oregano. Coat the vegetables with ½ cup olive oil and sprinkle with salt and pepper to taste. Cover and roast until the peppers and carrots are cooked completely and soft, about 12 minutes. Remove from the oven and deglaze the pan with the sherry. Place the sherry, vegetables, and chicken stock in a food processor and purée until smooth. Adjust the seasonings to taste.

To complete the dish, in a sauté pan heat the remaining ¼ cup olive oil over medium heat and sauté the shrimp. Turn the shrimp and add the sauce. Continue cooking until the shrimp are done, about 8 minutes. Fold in the mascarpone cheese and toss with cooked pasta (we use capellini, but most cuts will work well). Sprinkle with the fresh basil.

MAKES 2 TO 4 SERVINGS

Orzo con Anatra

(DUCK ORZO)

A luxurious dish that is rich, sweet, and earthy. Consider making it only when you can get good broccoli raab. Its tonic vegetable flavor is a brilliant balance for the opulence of duck and fruits.

2	(6-ounce) duck breasts
¼	cup olive oil
1	head broccoli raab, washed and chopped
1	medium Spanish onion, finely chopped
2	cloves garlic, minced
1	pound orzo pasta
2	cups chicken stock (see page 13)
½	cup dried cranberries
½	cup golden raisins
3	tablespoons toasted pine nuts
¼	cup (½ stick) butter
⅓	cup grated Romano cheese

Render the duck breast in an 8-inch sauté pan over medium heat until it is cooked through and the skin is crisp, about 5 minutes each side. Take the duck from the pan and thinly slice. In a 12-inch pot add the olive oil, preheat for 3 minutes on a medium flame and toast until golden brown. Add the broccoli raab, onion, and garlic. Stir in the orzo and cook for 5 minutes. Add the chicken stock and simmer for 15 minutes. Add the cranberries, raisins, pine nuts, butter, and cheese. Stir and serve.

MAKES 4 SERVINGS

Carbone's (above) has come a long way since 1961 (right).

Some of the people who make Carbone's what it is today: (L to R) Server Ann Vinci, Event Coordinator Mary-Beth Corraccio, Chefs Michael McDowell and Paul Rafala, Server Robin Mozille, Sales Assistant Ann-Marie Brodeur, and Bar Manager Bob Brodeur.

Once the favorite beer bar of Bulkeley Stadium ballplayers after a game (inset), Carbone's now serves fine wine to captains of industry.

Carbone's world-class wine cellar.

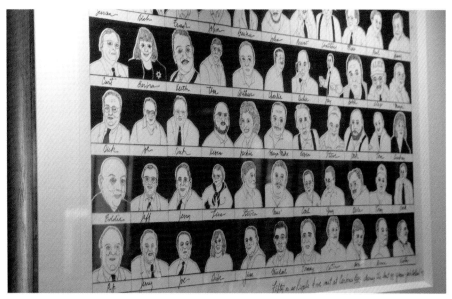

Many influential people visit Carbone's.

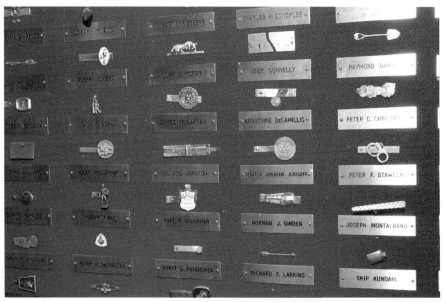

In 1963, to celebrate their silver anniversary Carbone's gave souvenir tie tacks to men (and pins to women). In return, some Broadcast Plaza executives gave their tie tacks to Carbone's, starting a trend that continues today.

Carbone's elegance abounds, without sacrificing welcoming service.

There is also entertainment with the flaming tableside preparations.

Guy Carbone seasoning his famous Steak Diane.

Steak Diane (page 124)

Orange Salad (page 20)

Fried Calamari (page 38)

Fried Eggplant (page 37)

Pasta Primavera, a seasonal favorite at Carbone's

Chilean Sea Bass (page 164)

Pumpkin Cake (page 194)

Cannoli Carbone

Risotto alla Paella

(RISOTTO "PAELLA STYLE")

This Italian gloss on the Spanish classic is a big, wonderful meal built upon risotto rather than traditional rice. It demands a robust red wine on the side.

¼	cup olive oil
1	medium onion, chopped
2	teaspoons minced garlic
6	ounces Italian sausage, crumbled
8	ounces boneless chicken breast, diced
6	ounces broken shrimp
6	ounces scallops
¾	cup arborio rice
2	cups chicken stock (see page 13)
1	head escarole, torn into bite-size pieces
⅓	pound oyster mushrooms, chopped
8	ounces mascarpone cheese
¼	pound Romano cheese, grated
8	leaves fresh basil, sliced
¼	pound unsalted butter

In a 12-quart saucepan heat over a medium flame the olive oil and add the onion, garlic, sausage, chicken, shrimp, and scallops. Sauté and stir for 5 minutes. Add the rice and chicken stock, stir for 10 minutes, and add the escarole, mushrooms, cheeses, basil, and butter. Stir for 5 minutes and serve.

MAKES 4 SERVINGS

Risotto alla Aragosta e Asparagi

(Lobster and Asparagus Risotto)

You can get lobster tails year-round, but this dish ought to be made only in the spring, when firm, flavorful asparagus starts showing up in the produce aisle. The combination of buttery risotto and lobster is an inspired one. The asparagus adds a garden-fresh note to balance all that richness.

¼	cup virgin olive oil
1	medium onion, diced
1	pound asparagus (½-inch pieces)
12	ounces arborio rice
16	ounces clam juice
4	(4-ounce) lobster tails (out of shell)
2	ounces (about ¼ cup) fresh tarragon
8	ounces mascarpone cheese
¼	cup grated Romano cheese
¼	pound unsalted butter

Heat the olive oil in an 8-quart saucepan for 5 minutes. Add the onion and asparagus and cook until tender. Add the rice and clam juice, stirring constantly for approximately 10 minutes. Add the lobster, tarragon, mascarpone cheese, Romano cheese, and butter. Stir for 5 minutes and serve.

MAKES 4 SERVINGS

Ravioli di Ricotta

(RAVIOLI WITH RICOTTA)

The simplest possible ravioli are wonderful when served warm with nothing but a veil of melted butter. For a heartier meal, Bolognese sauce is just the ticket.

PASTA DOUGH:

4   *cups all-purpose flour*

1   *tablespoon water*

3   *eggs, beaten*

RICOTTA FILLING:

1   *pound ricotta cheese*

1   *egg, beaten*

    Salt and pepper

¼   *cup grated Parmesan cheese*

2   *tablespoons fresh parsley, chopped*

To make the pasta dough, mix the flour, water, and eggs together and work into a firm dough. Cut into two balls and then roll each ball into thin sheets.

To make the ricotta filling, mix the ricotta cheese, egg, salt and pepper, Parmesan cheese, and parsley thoroughly and place large tablespoons of this mixture 2 inches apart on the sheet of dough. Place the second sheet of dough on the first, pressing dough around each mound and cut into squares. Press each cut edge of the squares to secure the filling. Cook the squares in salted boiling water for 15 to 20 minutes. Ravioli may be served with tomato sauce, butter sauce, or a Bolognese sauce.

MAKES 4 TO 6 SERVINGS

Maccheroni con Melanzane al Forno

(BAKED EGGPLANT AND MACARONI)

It's a Sicilian tradition to combine eggplant and pasta, the best-known version of which is Spaghetti alla Norma, after a Bellini opera. Carbone's version is made with ziti. It is a robust casserole reminiscent of lasagna.

1	medium eggplant, diced
	Salt
	Flour for dredging
1	clove garlic
4	ounces olive oil
1	pound ziti macaroni
6	ounces ricotta cheese
1	tablespoon pesto
1	plus 1 plus 1 cups tomato sauce (see page 66)
6	ounces mozzarella cheese plus some for topping
½	cup grated Parmesan cheese

Sprinkle the eggplant with the salt and drain with a weight on top of the eggplant for 30 minutes. Dry with a towel and dust with the flour. Fry the garlic in the oil until brown, remove the garlic, and fry the eggplant until tender. Cook the macaroni, drain, and mix with the ricotta cheese, pesto, and 1 cup of the sauce. Preheat the oven to 400°F. Place half of the macaroni in a baking casserole with half the eggplant, 1 cup tomato sauce, and half the mozzarella cheese. Repeat the procedure. Top with the remaining 1 cup sauce, grated cheese, and mozzarella cheese and bake for 15 minutes.

MAKES 4 SERVINGS

Linguine alla Vongole

(LINGUINE AND CLAM SAUCE)

Most Italian-American restaurants offer clam sauce for pasta, but in the Northeast, in Connecticut especially, it is an overwhelming favorite. Fresh cherrystone clams have a sweet marine flavor and tender flesh that seems to be a perfect match with al dente linguine . . . always with plenty of garlic.

30	cherrystone clams
½	cup olive oil
2	cloves garlic
¼	cup dry sherry
4	tablespoons chopped fresh parsley
	Freshly ground black pepper
2	tablespoons butter
1	pound linguine, cooked al dente

Wash and clean the clams. Put them in a stockpot, cover, and steam open. Chop the clams, strain, and reserve the liquids. Heat the oil in a saucepan, brown the garlic, and discard the garlic. Add the clams, sherry, reserved clam liquid, parsley, and ground pepper to taste. Cook for 2 minutes. Add the butter and serve over linguine.

MAKES 4 SERVINGS

Pasta alla Marzi

(PASTA MARZI)

Guy's friend Jim Marzi loved escargots, and in the 1970s when the family opened Gaetano's restaurant in the Hartford Civic Center, Guy came up with this dish to make him happy.

1	pound linguine
¼	cup olive oil
4	minced and 16 whole escargots
2	tablespoons minced onion
2	teaspoons chopped parsley
4	anchovy fillets
6	pimientos, chopped
	Milled black pepper
¼	cup breadcrumbs
1	tablespoon chopped walnuts
¼	cup grated Romano cheese

In a saucepot bring 3 quarts of water to a rapid boil. Cook the pasta until al dente, about 8 to 10 minutes. (A little vegetable oil in the water prevents the pasta from sticking together.) While the pasta is cooking, in a skillet heat the oil over medium heat. Add the minced escargots, onion, parsley, anchovies, pimientos, and 16 remaining whole escargots to the skillet. Sprinkle with the black pepper to taste and sauté for 2 to 3 minutes. Mix the pasta with the sauce and sprinkle with the breadcrumbs, walnuts, and Romano cheese.

MAKES 4 SERVINGS

Tagliatelle Verdi con Coteghino di Maiale

(GREEN NOODLES WITH HOG JOWLS)

Here is another recipe from the old days, when it was a matter of pride for cooks to take lowly cuts of meat and turn them into delicious meals.

4	hog jowls
1	teaspoon fennel seeds
1	bunch parsley leaves, chopped
¼	cup grated Romano cheese
1	clove garlic, minced
	Salt and pepper
4	pieces link Italian sausage
1	tablespoon olive oil
1	celery stalk, diced
1	small onion, diced
1	medium carrot, diced
½	cup white wine
2	(29-ounce) cans tomatoes (about 3½ cups each)
1	to 1½ pounds green noodles
	Simple Tomato Sauce (see page 66)
	Grated Parmesan cheese for topping

Sprinkle each jowl with the fennel seeds, parsley, cheese, garlic, and salt and pepper to taste. Place each jowl on a link of sausage and roll and tie it with a toothpick or string. In a saucepan over medium heat, brown the pork jowls in olive oil and add the celery, onion, carrot, and wine; allow the wine to evaporate. Add the tomatoes, cover, and simmer 1 hour and 30 minutes until done. Cook the green noodles, drain, and serve with slices of the jowls and tomato sauce. Top with Parmesan cheese.

MAKES 6 SERVINGS

Fettuccine d' Alfredo

(FETTUCCINI ALFREDO)

This is a very popular dish originally created by Roman restaurateur Alfredo di Lello back in the 1920s. Ribbon-shaped fettuccine are the traditional pasta, but other noodles may be used in their place.

24	*ounces fettuccini (or other noodles)*
¼	*cup (½ stick) butter*
½	*cup heavy cream*
1	*cup grated Parmesan cheese*
	Freshly grated black pepper

In a saucepot bring 5 quarts of water to a rapid boil. Cook the pasta until al dente, about 8 to 10 minutes. (A little vegetable oil in the water prevents the pasta from sticking together.) While the pasta is cooking, melt the butter and cream in a saucepan. Add the hot noodles to the melted butter and cream. Add the cheese and pepper and toss lightly until all the pasta is coated.

MAKES 6 SERVINGS

Fettuccine alla Carbonara

(ROMAN-STYLE SPAGHETTI)

An old-country recipe perfected by Charlie Carbone, Fettuccine Carbonara used to be known as one of the restaurant's tableside extravaganzas. Now it is made in the kitchen, but it remains a signature meal. As for the name of the dish, which literally means fettuccine in the style of the coal miner, Vinnie speculated that, based on his family's surname, some of his ancestors must have been in the coal-mining trade way back when.

6	slices bacon, chopped
3	thin slices prosciutto, julienned
8	ounces sausage, crumbled
2	eggs, well beaten
1½	pounds cooked egg noodles
	Black pepper and salt
½	cup grated Parmesan cheese

Cook the bacon until crisp and remove it from the pan. Cook the prosciutto and sausage in the same pan and add the sausage, prosciutto, eggs, and some of the drippings from the pan to the noodles. Serve with the black pepper and salt to taste and top with chopped bacon and grated Parmesan.

MAKES 4 SERVINGS

Pasta di Francesco

(FRANCESCO'S PASTA)

One day back in the 1970s, Kelly D'Aprile of D&D Market called Guy at the restaurant and asked his help. D'Aprile found himself with twenty-five pounds of sun-dried tomatoes that nobody wanted. At that time, few cooks knew about pumate (sun-dried tomatoes), which have since become an Italian-kitchen staple. Guy was interested and took the tomatoes from his friend. He used them to create Pasta de Francisco, the first restaurant dish in the area to make use of sun-dried tomatoes.

2	tablespoons chopped onion
1	teaspoon chopped garlic
2	anchovy fillets
4	teaspoons olive oil
½	cup sun-dried tomatoes
1	cup sliced mushrooms
2	ounces chopped prosciutto
¼	cup chicken stock (see page 13)
1	teaspoon basil pesto
1	pound pasta, cooked
2	teaspoons ricotta cheese
½	cup grated Parmesan cheese

Sauté the onion, garlic, and anchovy fillets in olive oil over medium heat. Add the tomatoes, mushrooms, and prosciutto and cook until tender. Add the chicken stock and pesto and toss with the pasta, ricotta, and grated Parmesan cheese to serve.

MAKES 4 SERVINGS

Pasta Panatula

(PASTA PANATULA)

In the early 1980s, Carbone's branched out from its old location in the South End and opened Gaetano's downtown. The restaurant was a showcase for Guy's inventive ways with Italian fare; this was its signature pasta.

1	pound pasta
6	ounces broccoli raab (about 2 cups chopped)
¼	cup virgin olive oil
1	teaspoon chopped garlic
	Hot pepper seeds
	Salt and pepper
¼	cup julienned roasted red pepper
4	ounces (1 cup) grated Romano or Parmesan cheese

In a saucepan bring 5 quarts of water to a rapid boil. Cook the pasta until al dente, about 8 to 10 minutes. (A little vegetable oil in the water prevents the pasta from sticking together.) While the pasta is cooking, steam the broccoli raab. Chop it and drain it well. Place it in a large pan with the oil, garlic, and pepper seeds and salt and pepper to taste. Add the roasted red pepper. Toss with the pasta and grated cheese.

MAKES 4 SERVINGS

Come Fare la Pasta

(BASIC PASTA DOUGH)

Italy's cuisines differ dramatically from region to region, but there is one constant no matter where you go: pasta. This basic recipe is for what Italian cooks call pasta all'uovo, meaning the dough is enriched by eggs. Carbone's suggests that a firmer dough can be made by substituting a cup of semolina for one of the four cups of all-purpose flour.

4	cups all-purpose flour
1	tablespoon water or a little more
3	eggs, beaten
1	teaspoon virgin olive oil
	Pinch of salt

Mix all the ingredients together and work into a firm dough. Let the dough sit for 30 minutes. Cut into two balls and roll each ball into a thin sheet of dough. Cut the dough into desired shapes. You can refrigerate it in an airtight container for 1 day, or you can freeze it indefinitely.

MAKES ABOUT 6 SERVINGS OF DOUGH

Note: Fresh pasta takes less time to cook than packaged. Be sure to check regularly until it is cooked al dente.

Cannelloni Gaetano alla Piedmontese

(GAETANO'S CANNELLONI PIEDMONTESE)

Aunt Billie is said to have been a master crêpe maker. "Hers were so light and airy," Vinnie says. They are a fine, subtle wrap for this meaty version of manicotti.

CRÊPE BATTER:

6   *eggs*

3   *cups water*

½   *teaspoon salt*

3   *cups all-purpose flour*

STUFFING:

2   *cups ricotta cheese*

2   *cups cooked sausage*

5   *tablespoons grated Parmesan cheese*

1   *egg*

     Salt and pepper

1   *tablespoon pesto (optional)*

     Tomato sauce (see page 66)

To make the crêpes, beat the eggs, water, and salt together. Add the flour to the mixture and stir gently to mix. Heat a 6-inch, nonstick fry pan to medium. Pour just enough batter in the pan to cover the bottom. Cook the crêpes for about 1 minute per side. Repeat until all the batter is used. (It should make 12 to 16 crêpes.)

To prepare the stuffing, mix the ricotta cheese, sausage, Parmesan cheese, egg, salt and pepper to taste, and pesto together.

To assemble the dish, divide the stuffing among the crêpes, completely using up all the stuffing. Spread the stuffing around and roll each crêpe like a jelly roll. Place them in a buttered casserole and cover with the tomato sauce. Bake 10 minutes.

MAKES 12 TO 16 SERVINGS

95

Cannelloni Gaetano alla Napoletana

(GAETANO'S CANNELLONI NEAPOLITAN)

These swanky main-course crêpes were originally served by Guy Carbone at Gaetano's restaurant in Hartford's Civic Center. They are a luscious combination of meats baked under a blanket of béchamel and cheese.

CRÊPES:

6	eggs
3	cups water
½	teaspoon salt
3	cups flour

FILLING MIXTURE:

1	cup cooked ground beef
1	cup chopped cooked chicken
½	cup chopped prosciutto
2	cups cooked and strained spinach, chopped
¼	teaspoon ground nutmeg
¼	cup grated Parmesan cheese, plus extra for topping
1	teaspoon chopped parsley
2	eggs, beaten
	Salt and pepper
	Béchamel sauce*

To make the crêpes, beat the eggs, water, and salt together. Add the flour and mix thoroughly. Heat a 6-inch, nonstick fry pan to medium. Pour just enough batter in the pan to cover the bottom. Cook the crêpes for about 1 minute per side. Repeat until all the batter is used. (It should make 12 to 16 crêpes.)

To make the filling mixture, preheat the oven to 350°F. Combine the beef, chicken, ham, spinach, nutmeg, Parmesan cheese, and parsley. Add the eggs and mix well and salt and pepper to taste. Divide the mixture among the crêpes. Spread the mixture on the crêpes and roll them up like burritos. Butter a baking pan and arrange the filled crêpes. Spoon on the béchamel sauce and sprinkle with Parmesan cheese. Bake for 10 to 12 minutes.

MAKES 12 TO 14 SERVINGS

*Note: To make the béchamel sauce, heat 2 tablespoons butter and combine with 2 tablespoons flour to make a roux. Add 1 cup of milk and simmer until of desired thickness.

• VEAL •

(Vitello)

Milan-Style Veal
Parmesan-Style Veal
Veal Birds
Carbone-Style Veal
French-Style Veal
Veal Scaloppine Marsala
Veal Durost
Veal Zingarelli
Veal of Love
Gaetano's Stuffed Veal
Veal Stew
Veal Sorrentino
Sliced Veal
Veal Pillows
Veal San Marino
Veal Pevari
Veal San Dominico

Vitello alla Milanese

(MILAN-STYLE VEAL)

Milanese (in the style of Milan) usually refers to meat that is dipped in an egg wash and seasoned breadcrumbs, then fried in butter. Veal cooked this way is an Italian restaurant staple—utterly simple, and utterly dependent on good-quality veal.

1½	cups breadcrumbs
¼	teaspoon salt
¼	teaspoon pepper
¼	cup grated Parmesan cheese
2	tablespoons chopped parsley
1	clove minced garlic
1	pound veal cutlets
	Flour for dredging
2	eggs, beaten
½	cup olive oil
	Lemon wedges for serving

Combine the breadcrumbs with the salt, pepper, cheese, parsley, and garlic. Very thinly slice the veal and pound it. Dredge the veal slices in the flour, dip them in the eggs, and roll them in the breadcrumbs mixture. Heat the oil in a saucepan over medium heat. Cook the cutlets in the oil until golden brown on both sides. Serve with lemon wedges.

MAKES 4 SERVINGS

Vitello alla Parmigiano

(PARMESAN-STYLE VEAL)

The "Parmesan" style of cooking things—dredged in seasoned flour, breaded and sautéed, then blanketed with tomato sauce and cheese—is virtually unknown in Italy. In America, it has become as much an Italian menu standard as spaghetti and meatballs.

1½	cups breadcrumbs
¼	teaspoon salt
¼	teaspoon pepper
¼	cup grated Romano cheese
2	tablespoons chopped parsley
1	clove garlic, minced
1	pound veal cutlets
	Flour for dredging
2	eggs, beaten
½	cup olive oil
	Tomato sauce (see page 66)
	Grated Parmesan cheese

Combine the breadcrumbs with the salt, pepper, cheese, parsley, and garlic. Very thinly slice the veal and pound it. Dredge the veal slices in the flour, dip them in the eggs, and roll them in the breadcrumb mixture. Heat the oil in a saucepan over medium heat. Cook the cutlets slowly in the oil until golden brown on both sides. Top with the tomato sauce and Parmesan cheese.

MAKES 4 SERVINGS

Involtini di Vitello

(VEAL BIRDS)

With its wine and vegetable sauce, this rolled and stuffed veal is a hearty winter meal, well accompanied by a brawny red wine. Italian preparation of veal frequently involves the use of seasoned breadcrumbs, the addition of spiced meats, and a touch of wine.

VEAL:		SAUCE:	
1	cup seasoned breadcrumbs*	1	clove garlic
1½	pounds veal, sliced	¼	cup olive oil
6	slices mortadella ham	2	tablespoons diced carrots
¼	cup olive oil	2	tablespoons diced onions
	Flour for dredging	2	tablespoons diced celery
		¼	cup Chianti wine
		1	tablespoon butter
		2	leaves fresh basil
			Black pepper and salt
		2	cups chopped tomatoes

Sprinkle the breadcrumbs on the slices of veal and place a slice of the mortadella on each. Roll and secure with a string or toothpick. Heat the oil in a large skillet over medium-high heat. Dredge the veal in the flour and brown in the skillet. Transfer the veal to a baking pan and set aside while making the sauce.

To make the sauce, brown the garlic in a pan over medium heat with the olive oil. Discard the garlic. Sauté the carrots, onions, and celery for 3 minutes; add the wine and butter and simmer for 2 minutes. Add the basil and the salt and pepper to taste. Add the tomatoes and simmer for ½ hour over low flame. Preheat the oven to 350°F. Cover the veal rolls with the sauce, cover the pan with aluminum foil, and bake for 30 minutes.

MAKES 4 TO 6 SERVINGS

*Note: You can season your own breadcrumbs by adding a small amount (¼ teaspoon) of salt, pepper, 1 cup Parmesan or Romano cheese, some parsley (1 tablespoon), and a little minced garlic.

Vitella al Carbone

(CARBONE-STYLE VEAL)

This is a special-occasion preparation for veal, made the way Vinnie remembers his mother and his grandmother cooked it.

4	slices prosciutto
4	slices provolone cheese
4	(8-ounce) veal cutlets
4	tablespoons all-purpose flour
2	eggs, beaten
1	cup seasoned breadcrumbs*
¼	cup olive oil
7	to 8 fresh sage leaves, chopped
4	to 6 ounces white wine
	Juice of ½ lemon
¼	cup butter
	Salt and pepper

Place a slice of the prosciutto and the cheese in each cutlet and fold. Press the edges with a fork. Dredge the cutlets in the flour, dip them in the beaten eggs, and press them into the seasoned breadcrumbs. Heat the oil and sage in a skillet over medium-high heat. Cook the veal until golden brown. After cooking, add the white wine and lemon juice. Cook for 2 minutes longer; add the butter and salt and pepper to taste and heat through. Pour the sauce over the veal.

MAKES 4 SERVINGS

*Note: You can season your own breadcrumbs by adding a small amount (¼ teaspoon) of salt, pepper, 1 cup Parmesan or Romano cheese, some parsley (1 tablespoon), and a little minced garlic.

Vitello alla Francese

(FRENCH-STYLE VEAL)

W hat we did differently in this 'Francese' was to add sour cream to the egg mixture," Guy Carbone explained. "It makes it richer and smoother."

4	tablespoons all-purpose flour
¼	teaspoon salt
¼	teaspoon pepper
1½	pounds sliced veal
4	eggs
1	tablespoon sour cream
1	tablespoon chopped parsley
1	tablespoon grated Parmesan cheese
2	tablespoons olive oil
3	tablespoons sherry
	Juice of ½ lemon
1	tablespoon butter
¼	tablespoon chopped parsley
12	slices lemon

Mix the flour with the salt and pepper and dredge the veal in the seasoned flour. Beat the eggs with the sour cream, parsley, and cheese. Dip the dredged veal into the egg mixture. Heat the oil in a large skillet over medium and fry the veal on each side. After cooking, discard the extra oil and add the sherry and lemon juice. Cook for 2 minutes longer, add the butter and parsley, and remove from the heat. Pour the sauce over the veal and serve with the lemon slices.

MAKES 6 SERVINGS

Scaloppine di Vitello alla Marsala
(VEAL SCALOPPINE MARSALA)

Veal Scallopine Marsala is customarily made with ordinary button mushrooms; but Guy pointed out to us that nowadays the global marketplace presents the adventurous cook with a panoply of ingredients once considered exotic. "Now you ask for mushrooms and you have a dozen different choices," he says. Still, he prefers using the old-fashioned button mushroom in this recipe.

4	ounces button mushrooms*
1½	pounds veal scalopine
½	cup all-purpose flour
6	tablespoons olive oil
	Salt and pepper
¼	cup Marsala wine
1	teaspoon soy sauce

Sauté and then drain the mushrooms. Dredge the veal in the flour. Heat the oil in a skillet over medium heat and sauté the veal for approximately 3 minutes. Add the mushrooms and sprinkle with the salt and pepper to taste. Add the Marsala wine and soy sauce and simmer for 2 minutes.

MAKES 4 SERVINGS

*Note: You may use a blend of your favorite mushrooms instead of button if you'd like.

Vitello Durost

(VEAL DUROST)

Veal Durost became part of the restaurant repertoire back in the late 1970s, when chef Tom Such came to the kitchen from the Johnson & Wales culinary school. The Carbones describe Such as "a very creative guy," evidenced here by the use of puff pastry and the combining of veal and seafood. "There's a lot going on here," Vinnie said of this recipe. "It's very 1970s."

SEAFOOD STUFFING:

2	cooked extra large shrimp, chopped
2	cooked mussels, chopped
2	cooked sea scallops, chopped
¾	cup (2 ounces) chopped mushrooms
1½	cups seasoned breadcrumbs
4	(5-ounce) veal cutlets
4	(5-inch) puff pastry squares

SEAFOOD SAUCE:

¼	cup (½ stick) real butter
4	cloves garlic, minced
¼	cup chopped onion
1	cup (4 ounces) sliced mushrooms
	Pinch of sage and white pepper
6	ounces extra large shrimp, chopped
4	ounces king crab, chopped
	Pinch of lobster base
	Pinch of roux
2	basil leaves, chopped
1	Roma tomato

Preheat the oven to 450°F. For the seafood stuffing, mix the shrimp, mussels, and scallops and add the mushrooms and breadcrumbs. Place the stuffing on the veal cutlets and fold them in half. Wrap the cutlets in the puff pastry. Bake for 18 to 20 minutes.

To make the sauce, melt the butter and brown the garlic. Add the onion and mushrooms and cook for 1 minute. Add the remaining sauce ingredients and simmer for 15 minutes.

MAKES 4 SERVINGS

Vitello Zingarelli

(VEAL ZINGARELLI)

Zingarelli was a customer who liked veal, sausage, and mushrooms; and it was for him that Guy created this dish. It has always been a practice at Carbone's to invent dishes based on customers' tastes and to name the dish for the customer who inspired it. However, sometimes the customer's name had to be changed a bit. Guy delights in saying that "If the person was Irish or Jewish and we made something for him, I'd remind him, 'This is an Italian restaurant. Do you mind if I add a few vowels to your name?'"

¼	*cup plus 2 tablespoons olive oil*
⅓	*cup chopped onion*
1	*cup chopped mushrooms*
6	*ounces veal sausage*
10	*ounces raw spinach, steamed, squeezed dry, and chopped*
3	*artichoke hearts, quartered*
½	*tablespoon grated Romano cheese*
1	*tablespoon grated Italian sharp cheese (Asiago)*
	Pinch of fennel seed
2	*pounds veal, thinly sliced into 2-inch pieces*
	All-purpose flour
¼	*cup sherry*
	Pinch of white pepper

Heat the 2 tablespoons oil in a skillet over medium heat and sauté the onions, mushrooms, and sausage together for 5 minutes. Add the spinach and artichoke hearts to the sausage mixture, making certain the spinach is squeezed dry. Add the cheeses and fennel seed to the mixture and blend well. Lightly dust the sliced veal with flour. Heat the ¼ cup olive oil over medium heat and sauté the veal, browning both sides. Add the spinach mixture, sherry, and white pepper. When cooked, top with Italian sharp cheese and put under the broiler until cheese is melted, approximately 1 minute.

MAKES 6 SERVINGS

Vitella Amore

(VEAL OF LOVE)

Veal Amore was originally created for Valentine's Day when a liquor company wanted Chef Jim Kehoe to make a new dish using Frangelico liqueur. Today Veal Amore remains a Valentine's special.

¼	cup olive oil
1½	pounds veal scallopine
	All-purpose flour
2	cups sliced mushrooms (about 12 ounces)
2	tablespoons chopped pimiento
8	chestnuts, chopped
2	tablespoons parsley
1	tablespoon butter
1½	ounces Frangelico
6	cups cooked wild rice

Heat the oil in a skillet over medium heat. Dust the veal in flour and sauté. Add the mushrooms, pimientos, and chestnuts and simmer for 4 to 5 minutes. Add the parsley, butter, and Frangelico and simmer for 2 minutes. Serve over wild rice.

MAKES 4 SERVINGS

TIE TACKS

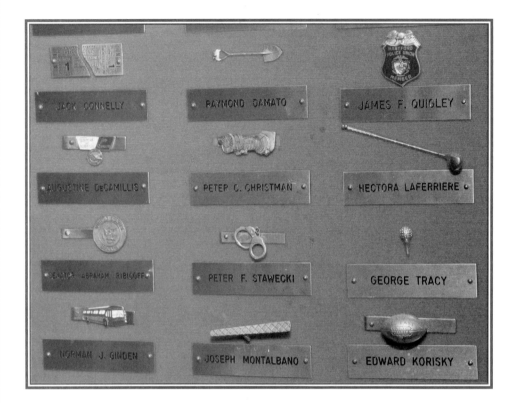

When Carbone's celebrated twenty-five years in business it was 1963, a time when nearly every self-respecting male who went to a nice place for lunch or supper wore a necktie. Fashionable gents wore skinny ties with front and rear aprons held together by a tie tack.

To thank patrons for their loyalty, the Carbone family decided to mark their silver anniversary by giving souvenir tie tacks to men (and pins to women). The motif on the gift was a crossed knife and fork—a logical symbol of a place to eat and a reminder, according to Carl Jr., that it was the Italians who introduced the fork to the world during the Renaissance. Broadcast Plaza executives Leonard Patricelli, Tom Eaton, and Robert Tyrol refused to take the gifts unless Carbone's accepted their own tie tacks in return. Tyrol explained that his father had brought him up to believe in the Swedish custom of acknowledging a gift by giving one back.

The three men's kindly gesture was the beginning of a long-standing tradition of regular customers bestowing Carbone's with tie tacks that symbolize their work and their interests. Today the walls of the restaurant are lined with cases filled with hundreds of tie tacks, no two alike, symbolizing the diverse men who have made Carbone's their favorite place for conducting off-site business, as well as raising glasses with friends. Many of the tie tacks displayed are personal coats-of-arms or insignias, and the signification of some is fun to figure out: handcuffs from a law-enforcement officer; a small gray rock from an executive at the Gra-Rock Ginger Ale Company; a #2 driver from a golf pro; a slide rule from an engineer; a 1966 *Hello Dolly* ticket from a backer of the Broadway show; one that the Carbone family describes as a replica of the millionth chip put in a Hitachi computer; and the Great Seal of the United States from former Connecticut Senator Abraham Ribicoff.

Gaetano Carbone remembers that the tradition brought one patron to the brink of divorce. He was so enthralled by the knife-and-fork he was given that he handed the restaurant his own pearl tie tack, only to return home to a wife who was livid at the exchange. She had given him the pearl tie tack for their own twenty-fifth wedding anniversary.

Vitello Imbottite alla Gaetano

(GAETANO'S STUFFED VEAL)

Another deluxe dish added to the menu by Guy Carbone, and frequently offered as a weekend special. It is a succulent spiral of veal and stuffing in a pool of natural juices.

7	pounds veal rib-eye
¼	cup olive oil
1	cup chopped onions
2	cups chopped mushrooms
8	ounces veal sausage
24	ounces raw spinach, steamed, squeezed dry, and chopped
2	tablespoons grated Romano cheese
2	tablespoons grated Italian sharp cheese (Asiago)
1	teaspoon fennel seed

Preheat the oven to 300°F. Prepare the veal by cutting and folding it into a flat sheet. In a skillet over medium-high heat, heat the olive oil and sauté the onions, mushrooms, and veal sausage for 5 minutes. Add the spinach to the sausage mixture, making sure the spinach is squeezed dry. Add the Romano cheese, Italian sharp cheese, and fennel seed to the mixture and mix well. Spread the stuffing mixture on the veal sheet and roll it up like a burrito. Tie it together and bake for 2½ hours. When cooked, let stand for 30 minutes before slicing. Serve au jus.

MAKES 12 TO 16 SERVINGS

Stufato di Vitello

(VEAL STEW)

Guy says that the secret of this dish is a long time simmering. Start with tender veal and sauté it in salt pork, then throw it in the pot with plenty of fresh vegetables. As it cooks, the meat absorbs the vegetables' sweetness and the veal's savor infuses everything.

1½	ounces salt pork, ground	¼	cup tomato purée
2	pounds veal, cut into pieces	½	bay leaf
	All-purpose flour	¼	teaspoon black pepper
¼	cup chopped celery	2	cups veal stock
¼	cup chopped onion	1	cup veal demi-glace*
¼	cup dry white wine	1	tablespoon chopped parsley
1	clove garlic, finely minced	¼	cup chopped cooked carrots
	Pinch of ground allspice		Flour and butter roux**

Cook down the ground salt pork in a large saucepan over medium-high heat. Dust the veal with the flour and brown with the salt pork. Add the celery, onion, and wine to the browned meat. Simmer for 10 minutes. Add the garlic and allspice. Add the tomato purée, bay leaf, black pepper, veal stock, demi-glace, and parsley. Reduce the heat and simmer for 3 hours. In the last 10 minutes add the cooked carrots. Add enough roux to the stew to thicken to your liking. The stew may be served over noodles, rice, or polenta.

MAKES 5 SERVINGS

*Note: To make the demi-glace heat veal stock and sherry until it is reduced and thickened enough to coat a spoon.

**Note: To make the roux heat 2 tablespoons butter in a saucepan and slowly stir in 2 tablespoons flour. Stir until the mixture gathers.

Vitello alla Sorrentino

(VEAL SORRENTINO)

A knife-and-fork "sandwich" of veal, ham, and cheese baked in a casserole. Quality of ingredients is especially important in this dish. You want good prosciutto and cheese, and of course you want tender veal.

1½	*pounds veal slices*
⅓	*cup plus 1 tablespoon olive oil*
4	*tablespoons butter*
¼	*pound fresh tomatoes, peeled and chopped*
2	*to 3 sprigs parsley, finely chopped*
1	*teaspoon oregano*
	Salt and pepper
12	*slices prosciutto*
12	*slices fontina cheese*
¼	*cup grated Parmesan cheese*

Flatten out the slices of veal. Heat 1 tablespoon of the oil together with the butter. Lightly fry the veal slices on both sides in a skillet over medium-high heat. Heat the remaining oil in another pan and add the tomatoes, parsley, oregano, and salt and pepper to taste and cook quickly for 10 minutes, or until the tomatoes are reduced to a pulp. Preheat the oven to 425°F. On each veal slice place a slice of ham and a slice of the fontina cheese. Spread with a tablespoonful of the tomato sauce and a generous sprinkling of the Parmesan cheese. Arrange the veal slices in one layer in a shallow baking dish and place in the oven until the cheese has melted, about 10 minutes.

MAKES 6 SERVINGS

Vitello alla Vincenzo

(SLICED VEAL)

At Carbone's, Vincenzo means scallopine of veal. The veal is stuffed with sautéed spinach and imported Danish Swiss cheese, dipped in an egg and sour cream batter, then sautéed until golden brown and served with a light mushroom sauce.

1	pound spinach, sautéed, drained, and seasoned with salt and pepper
8	slices Danish Swiss cheese
8	(6-ounce) veal cutlets
3	to 4 eggs, beaten
1	teaspoon freshly chopped sage
1	tablespoon sour cream
1	tablespoon grated Romano cheese
1	teaspoon chopped fresh parsley
	All-purpose flour
	Olive oil
½	cup white wine
¼	pound (1 stick) butter
¾	cup Madeira wine
2	teaspoons chopped prosciutto
	Salt and pepper

Place the spinach and cheese on the veal slices and fold in half. Combine the eggs, sage, sour cream, Romano cheese, and parsley to make a batter. Flour the veal lightly and dip in the batter. Sauté in the oil until lightly brown. Remove the veal and drain the oil from the pan. Deglaze the pan with the white wine. Add the butter, Madeira, and chopped prosciutto. Preheat the oven to 400°F. Place the veal in a casserole dish and pour the sauce over the veal. Bake for 5 to 8 minutes.

MAKES 4 SERVINGS

Cuscinetto di Vitello

(VEAL PILLOWS)

These pillowy veal pockets contain the vivid flavors of prosciutto and sharp cheese. The tang of artichoke hearts in sherry wine also helps create a beguiling aura around the gentle-natured veal.

4	(5-ounce) pieces veal
4	paper-thin slices prosciutto
½	cup seasoned breadcrumbs
1	cup shredded Italian sharp cheese (Asiago)
¼	cup virgin olive oil
1	cup all-purpose flour
½	cup sherry wine
1	teaspoon fresh lemon juice
8	grilled artichoke hearts
¾	stick (6 tablespoons) butter
	Salt and pepper

Lay out the veal pieces and top each with 1 slice prosciutto, 2 tablespoons breadcrumbs, and ¼ cup cheese and fold over. Heat the olive oil in a skillet over medium heat. Dredge the veal pieces in the flour and sauté for 3 minutes on each side. Add the sherry wine and lemon juice. Cook 2 or 3 more minutes. Add the artichoke hearts, butter, and salt and pepper to taste to finish the sauce. Pour the sauce over the veal.

MAKES 4 SERVINGS

Vitello alla San Marino

(VEAL SAN MARINO)

San Marino is a tiny island off of Italy that is in fact the third smallest state in Europe (after the Vatican and Monaco). Founded in the fourth century A.D., it is known to travelers for its excellent Italian food and local wines. Veal San Marino is doubly delicious because it contains both prosciutto and pancetta.

¼	cup olive oil
2	veal tenderloins, cut in half
¼	cup all-purpose flour
2	slices prosciutto di Parma julienne
4	slices pancetta, julienned
½	cup dry red wine
1	cup heavy cream
1	tablespoon crushed green peppercorns
2	tablespoons butter

Heat the oil in a large sauté pan over medium heat. Dredge the veal with flour and sauté for 10 minutes, turning constantly. Add the prosciutto and pancetta and cook until crisp. Remove the meat from the pan. Add the wine and simmer for 2 minutes. Add the cream and peppercorns, and finish with the butter.

MAKES 4 SERVINGS

Vitello alla Pevari

(VEAL PEVARI)

It's an inspired combination: gentle-flavored escalops of veal and sweet little bay scallops. Their quiet harmony is kicked up a couple of notches by a bright sauce of sherry, soy sauce, and hearts of artichoke.

1	cup all-purpose flour
	Salt and pepper
1	pound veal scallopine
⅓	cup virgin olive oil
½	pound bay scallops
4	grilled artichoke hearts
½	cup cooking sherry
2	teaspoons soy sauce
¼	pound (1 stick) butter
1	teaspoon chopped parsley

Flour and salt and pepper the veal to taste. Heat the olive oil in a skillet over medium heat. Sauté the veal for 2 to 3 minutes, turning once. Flour and salt and pepper the scallops to taste and add to the veal. Cook 3 more minutes. Add the artichokes, sherry, and soy. Reduce the sauce for 2 to 3 more minutes, turning over the veal and moving the scallops around. Right before serving, add the butter and chopped parsley. Stir well.

MAKES 4 SERVINGS

Vitello alla San Dominico

(VEAL SAN DOMINICO)

Here is a dish that combines the luxury of veal, cream, and porcini mushrooms. Made with cognac and marsala, it exudes an intoxicating aroma as it cooks . . . and when it is set on the table to eat.

1	cup all-purpose flour
4	(6-ounce) portions veal tenderloin, halved
3	eggs, whisked for egg wash
1	cup grated Romano cheese
⅓	cup olive oil
1	teaspoon minced shallot
½	cup Marsala wine
6	tablespoons (a little more than ⅓ cup) cognac
1	cup heavy cream
¾	stick butter
1	teaspoon dry porcini powder
1	teaspoon freshly chopped thyme
	Salt and pepper
6	to 8 ounces porcini mushrooms, washed and drained
1	teaspoon freshly chopped parsley

Flour the veal. Dip it in the egg wash, and then dredge it in the grated cheese. Sauté the veal in a nonstick pan in the olive oil until golden brown on each side. (It should be medium rare when served.) In a saucepan over medium heat sauté the shallot. Add the wine and cognac. Cook down to one-fourth of the volume. Add the cream and butter. Whisk well. Reduce this to less than half of the original volume. Add the porcini powder, thyme, and salt and pepper to taste. Cook to desired consistency. Add the drained porcini mushrooms and pour the sauce over the veal. Sprinkle with parsley.

MAKES 4 SERVINGS

ROMAN DINNER

When the Carbone family name was given to the restaurant in 1961, the second generation, Carl and Gaetano, had a clear and ambitious culinary goal: to redefine Italian food as something more than ordinary pizza and red-sauced noodles. They seized an opportunity when regular customer Joe Zieto came to them with a special request. Mr. Zieto said he was entertaining clients who were under the impression that Italian food was a plebeian plate of spaghetti and meatballs, and he wanted to prove them wrong.

Charlie, Tony, and Guy obliged by creating the "Roman Dinner," which became a long-standing Franklin Avenue tradition. Available only for parties of four or more and only if ordered in advance (and not on weekend nights when a busy dining room precludes leisurely service), this feast was designed to be the *ne plus ultra* of Italian cuisine. Like meals at the contemporary Forum of the Twelve Caesars restaurant in New York, Carbone's Roman Dinner evoked the splendor of the emperors and made the emphatic point that Italy's cuisine qualified with the best. It was a seven-course meal that began with cold antipasto and clams oreganato, included pasta carbonara, spinach or Caesar salad prepared tableside, sliced filet mignon, and concluded with Stregga liqueur-marinated fruits and/or a flaming dessert.

Writing about the Roman Dinner in a 1961 newspaper column, "New England Adventures in Dining Out," restaurant reviewer Hélène announced that such a meal at Carbone's was an opportunity "to go to Italy without a passport . . . an exciting adventure in dining."

· BEEF ·

(Carne di Manzo)

Pepper Steak
Gaetano's Stuffed Tenderloin Strip
Individual Stuffed Meatloaves
Steak Diane
Fillet of Beef Arrasto
Piedmont Beef
Beefsteak Ierna
Tenderloin Tips
Beefsteak with Gorgonzola Cheese
Beefsteak Cosenza
Sautéed Beef Tenderloin

Manzo al Pepe

(PEPPER STEAK)

Madeira wine sauce marks this dish as one contributed to the restaurant repertoire by a previous chef from outside the family. Neither Guy nor his father nor any other Carbone would normally make an extravagant Madeira sauce. Atop slices of beef tenderloin with fontina cheese, it is the crowning touch on one super-luxurious meal.

8	*(3-ounce) slices beef tenderloin*
4	*tablespoons olive oil*
1	*teaspoon chopped shallots*
⅛	*cup Madeira or Marsala wine*
2	*peppers, seeded, julienned, and roasted in oven until soft*
2	*teaspoons pesto*
¼	*cup veal stock*
1	*tablespoon butter*
	Salt and pepper
4	*ounces fontina cheese, sliced or grated*

Sauté the beef in the oil heated over medium heat. Drain the oil and add the shallots. Add the wine and simmer for 5 minutes to deglaze the skillet. Add the peppers, pesto, and stock. Reduce the sauce by half. Stir in the butter. Season with the salt and pepper to taste. Top the beef with the cheese, melt under the broiler, and serve.

MAKES 4 SERVINGS

Filetto di Carne Ripieno al Gaetano

(GAETANO'S STUFFED TENDERLOIN STRIP)

Guy explained that an efficient kitchen uses ingredients with multiple purposes. "You've got grilled steak on the menu, but here you also have stuffed steak. This way, you're less likely to wind up with groceries that go uneaten."

4	(6-ounce) beef tenderloin cuts
¼	cup cognac
¼	cup Marsala wine
4	slices bacon (optional)
	Salt and pepper
1½	cups seasoned breadcrumbs
4	slices prosciutto
12	slices provolone cheese
1	cup sliced mushrooms, sautéed

MUSHROOM SAUCE:

¼	cup cognac
¼	cup Marsala wine
6	ounces whole mushrooms
¾	cup butter
1	teaspoon soy sauce

Flatten each tenderloin with a mallet. Rub each piece with the cognac and wine. Let them marinate for 1 hour. Fry the bacon until crisp and chop it into pieces. Preheat the oven to 325°F. Place the marinated beef flat on a table. Add the salt and pepper to taste. Sprinkle each piece with the seasoned breadcrumbs and place a slice of prosciutto, 3 slices of provolone, and ¼ cup sautéed mushrooms on top and roll like jelly rolls. Skewer the tenderloins (use toothpicks to hold them in place), place in a baking pan, and cook for 45 minutes to 1 hour, or until done to your taste.

To make the mushroom sauce, while the beef is cooking, pour the wines into a saucepan over medium heat. Simmer until the wine is reduced by half or more. Add the whole mushrooms, butter, and soy sauce. Cook for about 6 more minutes. Serve over the cooked beef tenderloin.

MAKES 4 SERVINGS

Polpettoni Veronese

(INDIVIDUAL STUFFED MEATLOAVES)

Guy describes this polpettoni of ground beef and pork as an individual meat loaf, and a great thing to serve on a cold winter's day.

6	slices stale bread
½	cup milk
1	pound ground beef
1	pound ground pork
1	clove garlic, minced
2	tablespoons chopped parsley
2	eggs, beaten
½	cup grated Romano cheese
½	teaspoon salt
½	teaspoon pepper
3	hard-cooked eggs
6	slices mortadella cheese
¼	cup olive oil
	All-purpose flour
¼	cup Marsala wine
2	(28-ounce) cans diced tomatoes

Soak the bread in the milk, squeeze it dry, and add it to the ground meat. Add the garlic, parsley, eggs, grated cheese, salt, and pepper to the meat. Divide the meat mixture into six patties. Slice the hard-cooked eggs in half. Place 1 slice of mortadella cheese and half an egg on each patty. Close each into a large meatball. Heat the oil in a skillet over medium-high heat. Dust the meatballs in the flour and brown in the skillet. Place the meatballs in a large saucepan. Add the wine and tomatoes and simmer slowly for 45 minutes. Remove the meatballs and put the sauce through a blender or sieve. Serve the sauce over the meatballs.

MAKES 6 SERVINGS

Steak Diane

The beef industry says that Steak Diane was invented in the 1930s at the Copacabana Palace Hotel in Rio de Janeiro; but chances are good it existed before that. Named after Diana, the Roman goddess of the hunt and of the moon, it has become a signature dish of grand dining rooms where tableside presentation is a featured attraction.

2	tablespoons extra virgin olive oil
2	(12-ounce) sirloin steaks
½	cup all-purpose flour
2	to 3 shallots, chopped
3	to 4 mushrooms, sliced
2	tablespoons brandy
2	tablespoons Dijon mustard
½	cup beef broth
1	tablespoon butter
	Salt and pepper

Heat the olive oil in a large sauté pan over medium heat. Dredge the steaks in the flour and place in the sauté pan. Brown both sides of the steaks. Add the shallots and mushrooms and cook until the mushrooms are about half done, about 5 minutes. Add the brandy, mustard, and beef broth and continue cooking until the sauce is thick. When the sauce becomes thick, turn off the heat and stir in the butter until it is completely melted.

MAKES 2 SERVINGS

Filetto di Manzo Arrasto

(FILLET OF BEEF ARRASTO)

A specialty of Chef Paul Rafala, who, while he makes no claims to originating it, has well nigh perfected it—a complex presentation of beef stuffed with spinach, sweet sausage, and sharp cheese, and finished with a light Madeira wine sauce.

6	ounces veal sausage
1	tablespoon fennel seed
1	cup chopped onion
2	cups chopped, precooked mushrooms
¼	cup olive oil
24	ounces raw spinach, steamed, squeezed dry, and chopped
2	tablespoons grated Romano cheese
2	tablespoons grated Italian sharp cheese (Asiago)
6	(6-ounce) beef fillets, pounded to flatten
¾	cup Madeira wine
½	cup (1 stick) butter
2	ounces chopped prosciutto (about 4 slices)

Sauté the veal sausage, fennel seed, and onion in a large pan over medium heat; drain. Sauté the mushrooms separately in a small skillet in the olive oil and drain. Add the mushrooms and the spinach to the sausage mixture, making sure the spinach is squeezed dry. Add the Romano cheese and Italian sharp cheese to the mixture and mix well. Spread the stuffing mixture on the beef and fold over. Heat a little oil in a frying pan over medium heat and sauté the beef. Brown it on both sides. Add the Madeira wine, butter, and chopped prosciutto for garnish.

MAKES 6 SERVINGS

Tournedos Piedmontese

(PIEDMONT BEEF)

From the Piedmont region of Italy, this is a beef dish with a delicate character contributed by the rosemary and vermouth cream.

12	*(4-ounce) slices tenderloin, ¾-inch thick*
1	*cup all-purpose flour*
1	*tablespoon plus 1 teaspoon butter*
1	*tablespoon olive oil*
⅛	*teaspoon rosemary*
12	*green olives, sliced*
1	*teaspoon minced shallots*
½	*cup dry vermouth*
½	*cup heavy cream*
⅛	*teaspoon paprika*
	Salt and pepper
1	*teaspoon soy sauce*

Dredge the beef fillets in the flour. In a sauté pan heat the 1 tablespoon butter, olive oil, and rosemary over medium-high heat. Sauté the fillets, olives, and shallots for 3 minutes on each side. Add the vermouth and deglaze the pan. Add the heavy cream, paprika, and salt and pepper to taste. Lower the heat and simmer 2 minutes longer and remove the meat. Reduce the sauce by half and add the teaspoon of butter and soy sauce. Remove from the heat and pour the sauce over the tournedos.

MAKES 6 SERVINGS

Manzo Ierna

(BEEFSTEAK IERNA)

This elaboration of a basic scallopine includes fontina cheese, imported and domestic mushrooms, and pine nuts. It first appeared in the Carbone's repertoire some twenty years ago, when it was named for a regular customer named Mr. Ierna, for whom these ingredients were favorites.

4	*paper-thin slices prosciutto*
4	*(8-ounce) portions tenderloin flattened to ½-inch thickness*
1	*cup all-purpose flour*
¼	*cup plus 2 tablespoons olive oil*
4	*ounces shiitake mushrooms*
4	*ounces domestic mushrooms*
4	*ounces porcini mushrooms*
¼	*plus ¼ cup butter*
	Salt and pepper
8	*ounces fontina cheese*
1	*teaspoon pine nuts, browned*
⅔	*cup Marsala wine*

Preheat the oven to 400°F. Place the prosciutto on one side of the beef and then flour and sauté each side in 2 tablespoons olive oil until of desired doneness. Transfer the beef to a baking dish. Sauté the mushrooms separately in the remaining ¼ cup olive oil and ¼ cup butter until the mushrooms brown. Add the salt and pepper to taste. Add the mushroom mix, fontina cheese, and pine nuts to the beef pan. Deglaze the pan with the wine and reduce by half. Add the remaining ¼ cup butter, salt, and pepper. Pour over the beef. Bake for 4 to 6 minutes and serve.

MAKES 4 SERVINGS

Bistecchine alla Pizzaiola

(TENDERLOIN TIPS)

Add peppers and mushrooms to a beef dish and it becomes "pizzaiola." Here, beef tips bask with the vegetables and Marsala wine for just long enough to be kissed by their flavors.

1	tablespoon olive oil	1	large bell pepper, cut into strips
2	tablespoons butter	¼	cup sliced mushrooms
1	clove garlic	3	tablespoons Marsala wine
1¼	pounds beef tenderloin (cut into cubes ½-inch square)	¼	cup tomato sauce (see page 66)
1	medium onion, cut into strips		

In a large skillet heat the olive oil and butter over medium heat. Brown the garlic; discard the garlic. Sauté the beef in the oiled skillet. Add the onion strips, pepper strips, mushrooms, wine, and tomato sauce. Cook for 5 minutes and serve piping hot.

MAKES 6 SERVINGS

Manzo Gorgonzola

(BEEFSTEAK WITH GORGONZOLA CHEESE)

Few things in life are better than a good sirloin steak topped with creamy Gorgonzola cheese. Carbone's version adds the zest of anchovies and garlic.

¼	cup virgin olive oil	¼	teaspoon fresh rosemary
1	anchovy fillet	1	teaspoon chopped fresh parsley
1	teaspoon chopped garlic		Black pepper
6	ounces Gorgonzola cheese	4	(16-ounce) sirloin steaks
½	cup butter, softened		

Heat the oil in a small saucepan over medium heat. Add the anchovy and cook until dissolved. Add the garlic and sauté for 30 seconds to 1 minute. Add the cheese, butter, rosemary, parsley, and pepper to taste. Stir until a smooth sauce develops. Hold at room temperature. Grill the steaks to desired doneness and top with the Gorgonzola sauce.

MAKES 4 SERVINGS

Manzo Cosenza

(BEEFSTEAK COSENZA)

This is a beautiful thing to do with filets mignons if the flavor of the beef itself seems austere. Here it gets its culinary exclamation point from a combination of anchovies, shallots, garlic, tomatoes, and wine.

¼	cup olive oil
4	(5-ounce) slices filet mignon
¼	cup all-purpose flour
4	anchovy fillets
3	cloves garlic, minced
4	shallots, sliced
½	cup red wine
1	cup canned plum tomatoes, hand crushed

Preheat the oil in a 12-inch sauté pan over medium heat. Dredge the filets with flour and sauté for 3 minutes on each side. Add the anchovies, breaking them up in the pan. Add the garlic and shallots. Deglaze the pan with the red wine. Add the tomatoes and simmer for 5 minutes.

MAKES 4 SERVINGS

Manzo Sorrentino

(SAUTÉED BEEF TENDERLOIN)

This dish might also be called drunken beef, for although it isn't saturated with wine, the tenderloins do absorb maximum amounts of onion and mushroom flavor and the richness of butter.

1	teaspoon salt
1	teaspoon pepper
1	cup all-purpose flour
4	(8-ounce) slices beef tenderloin, cut in half
1	tablespoon olive oil
1	tablespoon butter
1	clove garlic
½	pound sliced mushrooms
½	cup chopped onions
¼	cup Marsala wine
2	tablespoons butter
1	teaspoon soy sauce

Mix the salt and pepper in the flour and dredge the slices of beef. Heat the olive oil and butter in a large skillet over medium heat and brown the garlic until golden; discard the garlic. Sauté the beef to your liking; then remove the beef from the pan and cover to keep warm. Sauté the mushrooms and onions until cooked to your liking. Return the meat to the skillet, adding the wine, butter, and soy sauce. Cook for 2 minutes.

MAKES 4 SERVINGS

· CHICKEN ·

(Pollo)

Chicken Sorrentino
Chicken Primavera
English-Style Chicken
Locario's Chicken
LaCava's Chicken
Chicken Diavola
Chicken Merango
Chicken André
Chicken Cacciatore
Chicken Saltimbocco
Chicken Cordon Bleu
French-Style Chicken

Petto di Pollo alla Sorrentino

(CHICKEN SORRENTINO)

There are a thousand versions of Sorrentino," Vinnie says. "It is a very, very savory dish, cooked with plenty of wine."

3	*whole boneless breasts of chicken*
¼	*teaspoon salt*
¼	*teaspoon pepper*
¼	*teaspoon sage*
¼	*cup all-purpose flour*
1	*clove garlic*
2	*ounces prosciutto, sliced into thin strips*
2	*cups mushrooms, sliced*
½	*cup sliced onions*
2	*tablespoons Marsala wine*
1	*tablespoon butter*

Place the chicken between sheets of wax paper and pound it thin. Slice into very thin slices. Dip the pieces of chicken into a mixture of salt, pepper, sage, and flour. Heat the oil in a skillet over medium heat. Brown the garlic and discard the garlic when browned. Sauté the chicken until brown and remove it from the pan. Add the prosciutto, mushrooms, and onions to the pan and cook until done. Return the chicken pieces to the pan and add the wine. Simmer for 5 minutes, add the butter, and remove from the heat.

MAKES 6 SERVINGS

Pollo di Primavera

(CHICKEN PRIMAVERA)

According to Guy primavera became popular in the 1970s and 1980s as people's diets began to change.

½	cup olive oil		1	cup diced tomatoes
	Juice of 1 lemon		1	onion, julienned
4	boneless chicken breasts, skin removed		1	cup packed spinach, chopped
			¼	cup peeled, julienned eggplant
SAUCE:			1	clove garlic
½	cup chicken stock (see page 13)			Black pepper
¼	cup sliced mushrooms			Dash of nutmeg
⅓	cup julienned carrots			Spicy mustard
⅓	cup julienned zucchini		4	hot cherry pepper

Mix together the olive oil and lemon juice. Pour over the chicken and marinate for 1 hour.

To make the sauce, heat the chicken stock in a large saucepan over medium heat. Sauté the mushrooms, carrots, zucchini, tomatoes, onion, spinach, eggplant, and garlic. Add the black pepper and nutmeg to taste. Cook for 3 to 4 minutes. (The vegetables should remain firm.) Preheat the oven to 450°F. Place the vegetables on a sheet pan. Spread the spicy mustard on the chicken and put the chicken on top of the vegetables. Bake for 25 minutes. Top with the hot cherry peppers.

MAKES 4 SERVINGS

Petto di Pollo Inglese

(ENGLISH-STYLE CHICKEN)

One of the all-time favorite chicken dishes at Carbone's, this one is still on the menu some forty years after Charlie invented it. Vinnie explains that the two-hour marinade not only tenderizes the chicken, but also brings out its flavor.

1	cup olive oil
4	plus 2 tablespoons sherry
1	clove garlic
1	teaspoon freshly ground black pepper
	Juice of 1 whole plus ¼ lemon
4	skinless, boneless chicken breasts
4	teaspoons prepared mustard
2	tablespoons butter

Combine the olive oil, 4 tablespoons sherry wine, garlic, black pepper, and juice from the whole lemon. Add the chicken and marinate for 2 hours. Remove the chicken from the marinade. Spoon 1 teaspoon mustard on the inside of each chicken breast; place them in a pan and broil for 8 to 10 minutes. Turn the chicken over and broil for another 5 minutes. Remove the chicken from the pan and pour off the excess oil. Add the butter, the remaining 2 tablespoons sherry wine, and the juice from ¼ lemon to the pan, stir, and pour over the chicken.

MAKES 4 SERVINGS

Petto di Pollo Locario

(LOCARIO'S CHICKEN)

This chicken dish, which includes ham and mozzarella and is topped with tomato sauce, is named after Angie Locario, sister of founders Charlie and Anthony Carbone and the first bookkeeper at the restaurant. "My mother was a great cook," Angie recalled. "She always helped with the sauce."

3	whole chicken breasts
	Salt and pepper
½	cup all-purpose flour
2	eggs, beaten
1½	cups seasoned breadcrumbs*
1	clove garlic
3	tablespoons olive oil
3	tablespoons butter
6	slices prosciutto or cooked ham
6	slices mozzarella cheese

Cut the chicken breasts in half and remove all the bones. Pound each breast under a sheet of wax paper. Salt and pepper the chicken to taste. Dredge each chicken breast in the flour; dip in the beaten eggs and then in the seasoned breadcrumbs. Brown the garlic in oil and butter and fry each breast on both sides until golden brown. Preheat the oven to 350°F. Place a slice of prosciutto and a slice of mozzarella cheese on each breast and cook in the oven for 10 minutes. Serve with a marinara sauce.

MAKES 6 SERVINGS

*Note: You can season your own breadcrumbs by adding a small amount (¼ teaspoon) of salt, pepper, 1 cup Parmesan or Romano cheese, some parsley (1 tablespoon), and a little minced garlic.

Pollo LaCava

(LACAVA'S CHICKEN)

Named for longtime family friend "Uncle" Roc LaCava, this dish combines two of Uncle Roc's favorite things to eat—sliced white chicken meat and veal sausage.

4	skinless chicken breasts, sliced into 1-inch pieces
	Salt and pepper
⅓	cup olive oil
2	large bell peppers, cut into eighths
4	stuffed cherry peppers, quartered*
2	shallots, chopped
2	(3-ounce) veal sausage links, sliced and baked or grilled
⅓	cup white wine
⅓	cup fresh lemon juice
⅓	cup softened butter

Season the chicken with salt and pepper to taste and sauté the chicken in olive oil over medium-high heat. Add the bell peppers, cherry peppers, shallots, and slices of veal sausage and cook for 2 minutes. Add the wine and lemon juice; reduce for 2 minutes. Remove the pan from the heat and add the butter. Pour the sauce over the chicken to serve.

MAKES 4 SERVINGS

*Note: Stuffed cherry peppers can be found in some grocery stores and in most Italian specialty stores.

Pollo alla Diavola

(CHICKEN DIAVOLA)

These chicken breasts stuffed with provolone cheese and seasoned breadcrumbs are served with a spicy sauce of pancetta bacon, crushed red pepper, and tomatoes. This is like chicken cordon bleu, but Italian-style (with provolone and pancetta) and hot. If you like your chicken less devilishly hot, use only a dash of crushed red pepper.

4	(8-ounce) skinless breasts of chicken
8	ounces provolone cheese
1	cup seasoned breadcrumbs*

SAUCE:

3	cloves garlic, crushed
¼	pound pancetta, diced
2	tablespoons olive oil
1	pound Italian tomatoes, crushed
¼	teaspoon crushed red pepper
¾	teaspoon black pepper
	Salt and sage

Preheat the oven to 450°F. Flatten the chicken breasts. Top with the cheese and breadcrumbs; fold in half. Bake for 25 minutes.

To make the sauce, brown the garlic and pancetta in the oil over medium heat. Add the tomatoes and cook for 45 minutes. Add the red pepper, black pepper, and salt and sage to taste and simmer for an additional 15 minutes.

MAKES 4 SERVINGS

*Note: You can season your own breadcrumbs by adding a small amount (¼ teaspoon) of salt, pepper, 1 cup Parmesan or Romano cheese, some parsley (1 tablespoon), and a little minced garlic.

Pollo Merango

(CHICKEN MERANGO)

After defeating the Austrians at Marengo, Napoleon was hungry. But provisions were low and because no butter could be found, his cooks made the chicken they were able to forage with olive oil. Napoleon is said to have liked the dish so much that he ordered it to be served after every battle.

⅓	cup olive oil
1	small onion, minced
1	tablespoon chopped parsley
1	cup chopped celery
1	clove garlic, minced
	Flour to dust chicken
1	chicken, about 3 pounds, cut into serving pieces
	Salt and pepper
2	small bay leaves
¼	teaspoon rosemary
¾	cup dry white wine
2	tablespoons wine vinegar
½	cup pitted green olives

Heat the oil in a skillet over medium heat. Sauté the onion, parsley, celery, and garlic gently until the onion is golden. Flour the chicken pieces and add to the skillet. Sprinkle with the salt and pepper and brown on all sides. Add the bay leaves, rosemary, wine, vinegar, and green olives. Cover and simmer for 35 to 45 minutes. Add a little water if necessary.

MAKES 2 TO 4 SERVINGS

WHERE THE ELITE MEET

The bar at Carbone's is open to all well-behaved, decently-dressed adult customers who walk in the door; but we don't know another public eating and drinking room that feels more clubby. Personal memorabilia from or about regular customers is posted on the wall, including caricatures of well-known patrons, and a general tone of quiet camaraderie gives the dark, comfortable room a privileged aura. If you walk in and perch on a stool at the bar or at one of the chest-high tables under the stained glass windows, you will find yourself in the company of politicians, business executives, real estate magnates, and other movers and shakers who come to this restaurant because it is a commercial and political sanctuary for making deals and planning the future of their part of the world.

Over the years, executives from major corporations have used Carbone's as a once-a-week lunchroom away from the office. Men's clubs have made the banquet rooms their meeting places. When Colt Manufacturing

Company was such a thriving concern that the land their vast plant occupied was known as Coltsville, executives met here for lunch several times a week. Today there is a whole board of tie tacks and lapel pins shaped like minuscule handguns and rifles—all from the men of Colt.

In the evening, you will likely see media and sports stars who come to relax and to be served by the family who has practiced hospitality for three generations. The gallery of signed 8 x 10 pictures in the vestibule includes head shots of singer Johnnie Mathis, Senator Chris Dodd, actor Dustin Hoffman, and quarterback Doug Flutie. Hartford Postmaster Laurie A. Timmons has her picture on the wall, as does Laycie Norris of the Dallas Cowboy Cheerleaders. Television personality Tom Poston wrote, "Guy & Carl: My taste buds misses youse guys. If you hang this, hang me high! I love a view."

Gaetano Carbone remembers the time singer Neil Diamond came in with his entourage and was kind enough to sign a tablecloth. Everyone was delighted, except Gaetano's Aunt Angie Locario, who has been a part of Carbone's since opening day in 1938. "Aunt Angie was furious," Guy laughed. "She said it showed no respect at all: 'Imagine, writing on a tablecloth!' she huffed."

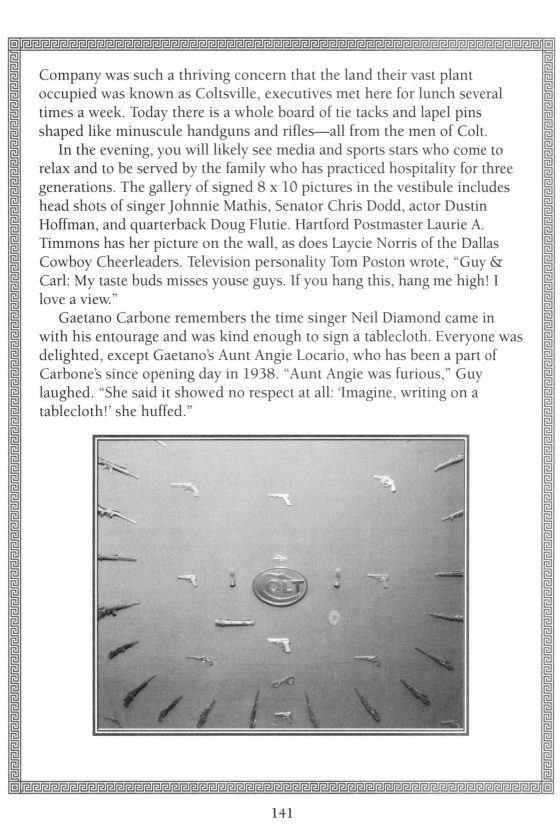

Pollo all' André

(CHICKEN ANDRÉ)

When Carbone's sister restaurant, Gaetano's, opened in the Hartford Civic Center in the 1970s, Chicken André was a featured menu item. Gaetano's was a high-end restaurant, as the copious crabmeat stuffed into these chicken breasts will attest.

4	*large boneless, skinless chicken breasts*
¼	*cup butter*
1	*clove garlic, minced*
1	*tablespoon chopped onion*
2	*tablespoons chopped celery*
¼	*cup white wine*
3	*cups seasoned breadcrumbs**
1	*pound crabmeat*
¼	*pound fontina cheese*

Preheat the oven to 325°F. Pound the chicken breasts flat with a meat mallet. Cook them for 10 minutes in the oven. Meanwhile, heat the butter in a skillet over medium heat. Add the garlic and brown. Add the onion, celery, and white wine and sauté for 5 minutes. Remove from the heat, add the seasoned breadcrumbs and crabmeat, and mix well. Stuff the chicken breasts with the crabmeat mixture and fontina cheese; fold over. Raise the oven temperature to 450°F and cook for 20 minutes.

MAKES 4 SERVINGS

*Note: You can season your own breadcrumbs by adding a small amount (¼ teaspoon) of salt, pepper, 1 cup Parmesan or Romano cheese, some parsley (1 tablespoon), and a little minced garlic.

Polla alla Cacciatore

(CHICKEN CACCIATORE)

Cacciatore is Italian for "hunter," and this term refers to a dish that is prepared hunter-style, meaning it contains mushrooms, onions, tomatoes, and usually wine.

½	cup all-purpose flour
¼	teaspoon salt
¼	teaspoon pepper
1	(2½ to 3-pound) chicken
¼	cup olive oil
2	cloves garlic
½	cup chopped onions
½	cup chopped mushrooms
½	cup chopped peppers
¼	cup sherry wine
2	cups tomato sauce (see page 66)

Combine the flour and salt and pepper. Disjoint the chicken and dust the pieces with the seasoned flour. Heat the oil in a skillet over medium heat. Brown the garlic and discard the garlic when browned. Brown the chicken in the oil. Once browned, remove the chicken and set aside. Sauté the onions, mushrooms, and peppers in the same skillet. Pour off any excess oil and add the chicken to the vegetables. Add the wine and tomato sauce and simmer for 15 minutes.

MAKES 6 SERVINGS

Pollo Saltimbocco alla Romano

(CHICKEN SALTIMBOCCA)

A dish for the veal-frowner: white-meat chicken breasts prepared in the same manner as veal for the classic Italian veal saltimbocca. Saltimbocca means "jump in the mouth." It is that good.

4	*(6-ounce) chicken breasts*
4	*slices prosciutto di Parma*
¼	*cup virgin olive oil*
4	*leaves fresh sage*
	All-purpose flour
½	*cup white wine*
⅓	*cup lemon juice*
2	*tablespoons soy sauce*
8	*ounces fresh mozzarella, sliced*
½	*cup softened butter*

Pound the chicken breasts until thin and press a slice of prosciutto on top of each breast. Heat the olive oil and the sage in a skillet over medium heat. Flour the chicken and sauté it for 3 to 4 minutes on each side. Add the wine, lemon juice, and soy sauce and cook for 2 to 3 minutes. Transfer the chicken to a baking dish and top with the mozzarella slices. Place the chicken under a broiler until the cheese melts. While the cheese is melting add the butter to the sauce. Cook the sauce until the butter is completely melted. Pour the sauce over each chicken breast before serving.

MAKES 4 SERVINGS

Pollo alla Cordon Bleu

(CHICKEN CORDON BLEU)

Cordon bleu literally means "blue ribbon," but in cooking, it refers to a classic preparation from the eastern regions of France in which thin slices of chicken (or often veal) sandwich prosciutto and Gruyère or other Swiss cheese, and the whole package is sautéed until it gets a light brown crunch on its exterior and the cheese inside is molten.

4	*(10-ounce) boneless, skinless chicken breasts*
4	*slices prosciutto*
4	*slices Swiss cheese*
1	*cup breadcrumbs for dredging*
½	*cup grated Parmesan cheese for dredging*
	Salt and pepper
	Mushroom Wine Sauce (see page 72)

Place each chicken breast between sheets of wax paper and pound flat. On one half of the chicken breast place 1 slice of prosciutto and 1 slice of Swiss cheese. Preheat the oven to 425°F. Fold the chicken over and flatten the edges together. Combine the breadcrumbs, Parmesan cheese, and salt and pepper to taste. Heat a skillet to medium-high heat. Dredge each breast in the breadcrumb mixture and fry each side to a golden brown. Place the chicken in a casserole and bake for 10 to 15 minutes. Remove from the oven and top with the Mushroom Wine Sauce.

MAKES 4 SERVINGS

Pollo alla Francese

(FRENCH-STYLE CHICKEN)

This "Francese" preparation is a little richer than Milanese (see page 149). It is more battered than breaded, and it is served with a wine and lemon sauce.

4	tablespoons all-purpose flour
1	teaspoon salt
1	teaspoon pepper
3	(10-ounce) chicken breasts
4	eggs
1	tablespoon sour cream
1	plus 1 tablespoon chopped parsley
2	tablespoons olive oil
3	tablespoons sherry wine
	Juice of 1 lemon
1	tablespoon butter
12	slices lemon

Preheat the oven to 375°F. Mix the flour and salt and pepper together and dredge the chicken breasts. Beat the eggs with the sour cream and 1 tablespoon parsley. Dip the chicken into the mixture. Heat the oil in a skillet over medium-high heat and sauté the chicken on each side. Transfer to a baking dish and bake for 10 minutes. While the chicken is cooking, discard the extra oil from the skillet and add the wine, lemon juice, butter, and the remaining tablespoon of parsley. Heat over medium heat for a couple of minutes. Serve the chicken with lemon slices and pan drippings.

MAKES 6 SERVINGS

· CHOPS ·
& GAME

(Costoletta & Cacciagione)

Gaetano's Stuffed Veal Chop Milanese
Grilled Veal Chop
Breaded Pork Chops
Breaded Lamb Chops
Lamb Shanks
Stuffed Turkey
Gaetano's Roast Pork
Venetian-Style Breaded Pork Chops
Broiled Lamb Chops
Rack of Venison
Rabbit Stew

Costoletta di Vetello alla Milanese di Gaetano

(GAETANO'S STUFFED VEAL CHOP MILANESE)

Milanese—in the style of Milan—usually refers to meat dipped in an egg wash and seasoned breadcrumbs, then fried in butter. These chops are stuffed with fontina cheese, and rather than being sautéed, they are baked until golden brown and served in a lemon-butter sauce.

6	veal chops, ¾-inch thick
4	ounces fontina cheese, cut into 6 portions
	All-purpose flour
2	eggs, beaten
3	cups seasoned breadcrumbs*
¼	pound (1 stick) butter
	Juice of 1 lemon
	Lemon slices for garnish
3	tablespoons chopped parsley for garnish

Preheat the oven to 450°F. Slice a pocket in each veal chop and place the fontina cheese in the pocket. Dust the chops with flour, dip in the eggs, and then dip in the seasoned breadcrumbs. Bake for 12 to 15 minutes. Melt the butter, mix with the lemon juice, and pour over the chops when ready to serve. Garnish with lemon wheels and parsley.

MAKES 6 SERVINGS

*Note: You can season your own breadcrumbs by adding a small amount (¼ teaspoon) of salt, pepper, 1 cup Parmesan or Romano cheese, some parsley (1 tablespoon), and a little minced garlic.

Costoletta di Vitello alla Griglia

(GRILLED VEAL CHOP)

This dish uses a very basic preparation of veal chops for which you want extra thick chops. Broiled and served with a sauce of porcini, wild and domestic mushrooms, pine nuts, cheese, and brandy, they become a celebration meal.

6	*veal chops, ¾-inch thick*

THREE-WAY MUSHROOM SAUCE:

½	*pound mushrooms (shiitake, porcini, & white mix), sliced*
4	*ounces pine nuts*
1	*tablespoon olive oil*
2	*tablespoons brandy*
½	*cup veal stock*
6	*tablespoons butter*
¾	*cup grated mozzarella cheese*
¾	*cups grated smoked mozzarella cheese*

Broil the veal chops for 12 to 15 minutes.

To make the mushroom sauce, sauté the three kinds of mushrooms. Pour off the extra liquid. In a separate saucepan sauté the pine nuts in the oil over medium-high heat until lightly browned. Add the mushrooms and brandy and cook for 10 minutes. Add the veal stock and butter. Mix with both mozzarella cheeses and let cool.

MAKES 6 SERVINGS

Costoletta di Maiale alla Veneziana

(BREADED PORK CHOPS)

Vinnie points out how many traditional Italian recipes use a vinegar marinade. This is to help bring out the flavor of the meat and also to tenderize it.

12	boneless pork chops
1	cup vinegar
1	clove garlic, minced
1	cup all-purpose flour
¼	teaspoon salt
¼	teaspoon pepper
3	eggs
¼	cup water
2	cups seasoned breadcrumbs*
½	cup olive oil

Marinate the chops in the vinegar and garlic for 1 hour. Combine the flour, salt, and pepper. Wipe the chops dry and dredge in the seasoned flour. Beat the eggs and water together. Dip the chops into the batter and then dip into the seasoned breadcrumbs. In a saucepan heat the oil over medium-high heat and sauté the chops until golden brown.

MAKES 6 SERVINGS

*Note: You can season your own breadcrumbs by adding a small amount (¼ teaspoon) of salt, pepper, 1 cup Parmesan or Romano cheese, some parsley (1 tablespoon), and a little minced garlic.

Costoletta di Agnello

(BREADED LAMB CHOPS)

My grandfather loved the simplicity of chops, just baked or sautéed," Vinnie says of Charlie Carbone. Here's how Charlie made chops.

8	*(4-ounce) loin chops*
1	*cup grated Romano cheese*
2	*eggs, beaten*
1	*cup seasoned breadcrumbs**
½	*cup olive oil*
	Lemon wedges for garnish

Thinly cut the chops. Remove the bones and any excess fat and pound the meat until flat. Press the chops into the cheese, dip them into the eggs, and press them into the seasoned breadcrumbs. Heat the oil in a saucepan over medium-high heat and sauté the chops until golden brown. Serve with lemon wedges.

MAKES 4 SERVINGS

*Note: You can season your own breadcrumbs by adding a small amount (¼ teaspoon) of salt, pepper, 1 cup Parmesan or Romano cheese, some parsley (1 tablespoon), and a little minced garlic.

Cosciotto d' Agnello

(LAMB SHANKS)

The lamb version of osso buco, served with a rich sauce. Wine vinegar adds compelling gusto to the earthy flavor of the lamb.

4	*(4-ounce) lamb shanks*
7	*to 9 garlic cloves*
2	*teaspoons chopped fresh parsley*
2	*teaspoons chopped fresh rosemary*
¼	*cup Parmesan/Romano cheese*
½	*cup wine vinegar*
1	*tablespoon prepared mustard*
	Salt and pepper

Trim off most of the fat and make several slits in each shank. Insert the garlic, parsley, rosemary, and cheese into the slits. Blend the vinegar, mustard, and salt and pepper to taste. Marinate the shanks in the mixture for 1 hour. Preheat the oven to 350°F. Place the lamb in a roasting pan and bake for 1 to 1½ hours. Keep basting with the marinade. Serve with dandelion greens or arugula and roasted potatoes.

MAKES 4 SERVINGS

Tacchino Arrosto Ripieno

(STUFFED TURKEY)

My father used to make stuffed turkey for us," Guy recalls. "It's almost like mozzarella in carrozza, but instead of bread, the 'carriage' around the ham and cheese is turkey." Although created decades ago by Charlie Carbone, stuffed turkey is still a popular special at the restaurant.

¼	teaspoon sage
12	(4- to 6-ounce) turkey fillets
6	slices prosciutto
6	slices mozzarella
1	cup all-purpose flour
¼	teaspoon salt
¼	teaspoon pepper
2	eggs, beaten
⅛	cup water
2	cups seasoned breadcrumbs*
¼	cup oil
	Mushroom Wine Sauce (see page 72)

Sprinkle the sage onto six of the turkey fillets. Place a slice of prosciutto and a slice of cheese on each seasoned fillet and cover with a second fillet. Combine the flour, salt, and pepper. Dust each sandwich-like fillet with the seasoned flour. Beat together the eggs with the water and dip the fillets into the egg mixture. Then press them into the seasoned breadcrumbs. Heat the oil in a saucepan over medium-high heat and sauté the fillets until golden brown. Preheat the oven to 375°F. Arrange the fillets in a single layer in a baking dish and bake for 10 minutes. Serve with Mushroom Wine Sauce.

MAKES 6 SERVINGS

Maiale Arrosto alla Gaetano

(GAETANO'S ROAST PORK)

For the pork lover, nothing's better than this mighty roast: pork stuffed with sausage and garlic with just enough provolone to help keep it all together.

4	to 5 pounds pork butts, boned
1	teaspoon fennel seed
2	tablespoons grated cheese
6	ounces sausage meat
2	cloves garlic, finely chopped
6	slices provolone cheese
	Parsley
	Mushroom Wine Sauce (see page 72)

Preheat the oven to 300°F. Roll out the pork. Season it with the fennel, grated cheese, sausage, garlic, provolone slices, and parsley to taste. Roll it up like a jelly roll and tie it together with string. Bake it for 2½ hours. Slice and serve topped with mushroom wine sauce.

MAKES 12 TO 16 SERVINGS

Costoletta di Maiale alla Veneziana

(VENETIAN-STYLE BREADED PORK CHOPS)

The vinegar marinade in which these pork chops bathe at the beginning of this process actually helps underline the sweet flavor of the pork. And if the chops themselves aren't quite porky enough for you, the diced bacon helps!

12	(6- to 8-ounce) boneless pork chops	1	onion, diced	
1	cup wine vinegar	2	peppers, diced	
	Salt and pepper	¼	pound bacon, diced	
	All-purpose flour	¼	cup butter	
3	eggs, beaten	½	cup tomato purée	
1½	cups seasoned breadcrumbs*	½	cup stock	
½	cup oil and butter mix	½	teaspoon fennel seeds	
1	clove garlic	2	tablespoons sherry	

Flatten the chops and marinate for 1 hour in the wine vinegar. Drain the marinade from the chops and season with salt and pepper to taste. Dredge the chops in flour, then in the beaten eggs, and finally in the seasoned breadcrumbs. Heat the oil and butter mix in a saucepan over medium heat. Brown the garlic; discard the garlic when browned. Turn the heat to medium high and sauté the chops until done and remove from the pan. Sauté the onion, peppers, and bacon in the butter for 5 minutes. Add the tomato purée, stock, fennel seeds, and sherry and cook for 30 minutes. Preheat the oven to 400°F. Place the chops in a casserole, cover with the sauce, and bake for 12 to 15 minutes longer.

MAKES 12 SERVINGS

*Note: You can season your own breadcrumbs by adding a small amount (¼ teaspoon) of salt, pepper, 1 cup Parmesan or Romano cheese, some parsley (1 tablespoon), and a little minced garlic.

Option: The chops may be baked in the oven for 15 minutes with the sauce served on the side.

Costoletta di Agnello Arrostito

(BROILED LAMB CHOPS)

Start with good lamb chops, and this light, sweet vegetable sauce—ineffably enriched by the flavor of lamb bones—will make them something divine.

SAUCE:

2	*pounds lamb bones*
½	*cup plus 2 tablespoons all-purpose flour*
3	*carrots, chopped*
1	*large onion, chopped*
	Salt and pepper
8	*cups (64 ounces) light chicken or beef stock*
2	*tablespoons butter*
8	*(1-inch thick) loin lamb chops*

To make the vegetable sauce, preheat the oven to 450°F. Place the lamb bones in a roasting pan and cover with the ½ cup flour. Bake in the oven until brown. Place the carrots, onion, and salt and pepper to taste in a stockpot with the chicken or beef stock and bring to a boil. Add the lamb bones to the stockpot. Let simmer for 2 hours. Make a roux by heating the butter and mixing together with the 2 tablespoons flour until it forms a paste. Strain the stock into a small saucepan over medium heat and thicken with the roux. Broil the chops for 5 minutes on each side. Serve with the vegetable sauce.

MAKES 4 SERVINGS

Costoletta di Cervo

(RACK OF VENISON)

The "Chef's Tour of Italy" is Carbone's way of offering guests an extra-special meal of dishes that reflect some of the less-known aspects of Italian cuisine. Farm-raised venison is used in this dish, always prepared with a great show tableside.

¼	cup olive oil
1	venison rack, cut into 8 chops
2	tablespoons coarse-ground black pepper
6	shallots, sliced
2	cups sliced fresh porcini mushrooms
½	cup Barolo (red) wine
1	cup demi-glace* (Knorr package is fine)
1	teaspoon Dijon mustard
1	teaspoon Worcestershire sauce
1	tablespoon butter

Heat the oil in a medium sauté pan over medium heat. Encrust the chops with black pepper and braise them in the pan for 4 minutes on each side. Add the shallots and mushrooms. Deglaze the pan with the red wine. Add the demi-glace. Add the mustard, Worcestershire, and finish with the butter.

MAKES 8 SERVINGS

*Note: To make the demi-glace heat veal stock that has been thickened with a brown roux and sherry until it is reduced and thickened enough to coat a spoon.

Coniglio alla Cacciatore

(RABBIT STEW)

In some ways, this is a more true-to-life version of the cacciatore—aka hunter's stew—that is more commonly made from chicken. This one uses rabbit, which has a lot of parts, so it is especially good to serve to people who enjoy worrying tender little pieces of meat from small bones.

3	pounds cleaned rabbit
3	cups red wine
2	tablespoons salt
	All-purpose flour
1/3	cup butter
1/4	cup olive oil
4	stalks celery, finely diced
2	medium onions, finely diced
2	teaspoons chopped parsley
	Salt and pepper
2	cups dry sherry
3	tablespoons tomato paste
1/2	cup black olives
1/2	cup Greek or Sicilian olives

Cut the rabbit into serving pieces. Place in a deep dish and add the red wine and enough cold water to cover. Add the salt and marinate for 4 hours. Dry with a paper towel and dust with the flour. Melt the butter and olive oil in a skillet over medium-high heat and brown the rabbit on all sides, about 10 minutes. Lower the flame and add the celery, onions, and parsley. Season to taste with the salt and pepper. Cover and simmer about 10 minutes. Blend the sherry and tomato paste and add gradually to the skillet, stirring frequently to prevent burning. Add both varieties of olives, cover, and simmer over low flame about 45 minutes or until the rabbit is tender. If necessary, add a small quantity of water to make more sauce.

MAKES 8 TO 10 SERVINGS

THE SOUTHERN PLANTATION MEN'S CLUB

Following World War II, many men who lived and worked on the South End considered a drink after work at the Southern Plantation to be an essential part of their day. At times that one drink turned into many, and a short visit became a night out. "At least one Friday per month we would wind up in an all-night poker game at one of the guy's homes," Uncle Roc LaCava recalls. "Then breakfast by the Weathersfield River, and for some of us, off to work."

It was during one of these all-night sessions that the guys first discussed the idea of forming a social club, which became a reality in 1950. The Southern Plantation Men's Club sponsored dances, Christmas parties for children, and banquets throughout the year. Uncle Roc remembers that its membership included "lawyers, a future judge, engineers, carpenters, masons, politicians, a future mayor, and many men who would advance in the corporate world."

In addition to gathering for drinks and good cheer at the restaurant, the men of the club regularly attended sports events together, traveling on special trains to games at Yankee Stadium and the Polo Grounds. "The two- or three-hour train ride was party time," Uncle Roc said. "There was ample food, and more than ample drinks."

· SEAFOOD ·

(Frutti di Mare)

Baked Stuffed Scampi
Chilean Sea Bass
Baked Fillet of Sole Milan Style
Conch and Squid Stew
Baked Sardines
Baked Fillet of Sole
Baked Stuffed Squid
Pan Fried Shrimp
Seafood Posillipo
Swordfish with Vegetables and Srimp
Shrimp Rocco
Pecorino Encrusted Swordfish
Swordfish Genovese Style
Cod "Garden" Style
Baked Fillet of Fish
Grilled Tuna
Baked Halibut
Spiced Shrimp
Fillet of Sole Florentine Style
Spicy Salmon with Artichokes
Salmon in Phyllo

Scampi Imbottiti al Forno

(BAKED STUFFED SCAMPI)

Scampi literally refers to the tail sections of prawn or lobsters. But on Italian-American menus, it almost always means shrimp . . . and plenty of garlic.

18	to 24 (size U-5) shrimp
2	cloves garlic, minced
2	teaspoons fresh parsley
1	tablespoon oregano
2	cups scampi breadcrumbs*
1	cup grated Pecorino Romano cheese
	Pinch of salt and pepper
½	cup virgin olive oil
	Lemon and drawn butter or Scampi Romance Sauce (see page 73)

Wash the shrimp and split on the underside. Lift from the shell and devein; replace in the shell.

Preheat the oven to 400°F. Mix the garlic with the parsley and oregano. Add the breadcrumbs, cheese, salt, pepper, and oil and mix thoroughly. Place the stuffing on each shrimp and bake for 15 to 20 minutes. Serve with lemon and drawn butter or serve with Scampi Romance Sauce.

MAKES 6 SERVINGS

*Note: To make the scampi breadcrumbs combine 2 cups breadcrumbs with 1 cup Romano cheese, 4 teaspoons chopped parsley, 6 minced garlic cloves, and ½ teaspoon black pepper. Add some olive oil to moisten and a couple teaspoons of oregano.

Spigola alla Cilena

(CHILEAN SEA BASS)

To our knowledge, Chilean Sea Bass did not exist on any menu before a couple of decades ago. It has since become a favorite dish in restaurants of all ethnic persuasion. Formally known as Patagonian toothfish, it is popular because its flesh is fairly fatty, meaning it can be broiled or grilled without getting dry. Carbone's sautées it and offers it as the centerpiece of a grand Italian main course.

1	tablespoon paprika	1	(3-ounce) slice of rind from prosciutto di Parma
1	tablespoon curry		
1	teaspoon cumin	1	large carrot, diced
½	teaspoon black pepper	1	large Spanish onion, diced
½	teaspoon chopped garlic	6	stalks celery, diced
½	teaspoon chopped fresh tarragon	1	(10-ounce) can cannellini beans
		½	cup peeled, crushed tomatoes
4	(8-ounce) sea bass fillets	1	tablespoon basil pesto or fresh basil leaves
2	plus 2 tablespoons virgin olive oil		
3	tablespoons butter	2	cups veal stock
3	tablespoons flour		

Preheat the oven to 350°F. Combine the paprika, curry, cumin, black pepper, garlic, and tarragon. Dredge the fish fillets in the herb/spice mixture. Heat 2 tablespoons of oil in a skillet over medium-high heat. Sauté the fish on both sides until golden in color. Finish in the oven for 10 minutes until cooked through. Make a roux by melting the butter in a small skillet over medium heat. Add the flour and stir until it forms a paste. In a 4-quart saucepan heat the remaining 2 tablespoons oil and pan-sear the prosciutto. Add the carrot, onion, and celery; sauté until tender. Add the beans, tomatoes, basil, and veal stock. Thicken with the roux. After taking the fish out of the oven, top it with the sauce. You may want to dress the dish with a drizzling of aged balsamic vinegar and virgin olive oil and garnish it with watercress.

MAKES 4 SERVINGS

Filetto di Sogliola alla Milanese

(BAKED FILLET OF SOLE MILAN STYLE)

The name of this recipe sounds exotic. In fact, it is one of the simplest and best things to do with a few good pieces of fresh fillet of sole: sauté, drizzle with butter, then bake. And serve with nothing more than a spritz of lemon.

1¼	cups sliced onion
2	tablespoons olive oil
1	bay leaf
½	teaspoon salt
½	teaspoon pepper
¼	cup sauterne wine
6	(7-ounce) sole fillets
	All-purpose flour
2	eggs, beaten
1½	cups seasoned breadcrumbs*
2	tablespoons melted butter
	Lemon slices

Preheat the oven to 350°F. Sauté the onion in the olive oil over medium-high heat until translucent. Add the bay leaf, salt, pepper, and sauterne. Simmer until the sauterne evaporates (about 2 minutes) and place in the bottom of a baking casserole. Dredge the sole in the flour, dip in the eggs, and press into the breadcrumbs. Place the fish in the casserole, drizzle with the butter, and bake for 10 minutes. Serve with lemon slices.

MAKES 6 SERVINGS

*Note: You can season your own breadcrumbs by adding a small amount (¼ teaspoon) of salt, pepper, 1 cup Parmesan or Romano cheese, some parsley (1 tablespoon), and a little minced garlic.

Stufato di Conchiglia e Calamari

(CONCH AND SQUID STEW)

This aromatic dish can be a main course served with bruschetta or just lengths of crusty bread for dipping and mopping. It also makes a great topping for linguine or other ribbon-shaped pasta.

1	*pound conch meat*
1	*pound cleaned squid*
¼	*cup olive oil*
1	*clove garlic*
½	*cup chopped onion*
¼	*cup chopped celery*
¼	*cup sherry wine*
1	*cup chopped tomatoes*
	Salt and pepper
¼	*teaspoon oregano*
½	*blade bay leaf*
¼	*teaspoon basil*
¼	*teaspoon hot pepper seeds (optional)*

Slice the conch and squid into 1-inch pieces. Heat the oil in a skillet over medium heat, brown the garlic, and then discard the garlic. Sauté the onion, celery, and fish for 5 minutes. Add the wine and reduce by half. Add the tomatoes and simmer for ½ hour. Add the salt and pepper to taste, oregano, bay leaf, basil and seeds, if using, and simmer for 5 minutes. This dish is often served with linguine or as a stew with bruschetta.

MAKES 4 TO 6 SERVINGS

Sarde al Forno

(BAKED SARDINES)

Sardines are moist, full-flavored little fish. Baked with a little cheese, garlic, and oil until just a bit crunchy, they make a wonderful snack. Serve hot from the oven with wedges of lemon to squeeze.

2	*pounds sardines*
½	*cup breadcrumbs*
2	*tablespoons grated Parmesan cheese*
1	*teaspoon oregano*
¼	*teaspoon salt*
1	*teaspoon pepper*
¼	*clove garlic, minced*
2	*tablespoons olive oil*
	Lemon slices

Clean and remove the sardine heads. Place the sardines in a greased baking pan. Preheat the oven to 400°F. Mix the breadcrumbs, cheese, oregano, salt, pepper, and garlic thoroughly and sprinkle on the fish. Sprinkle the olive oil over the breadcrumb mixture and bake for 15 minutes. Serve with lemon slices.

MAKES 6 SERVINGS

Filetti di Sogliola al Forno

(BAKED FILLET OF SOLE)

Carbone's dresses up its fillet of sole by blanketing it with a bright mixture of prosciutto, cheese, and breadcrumbs, then baking it (with butter, of course) until the crumbs begin to brown.

¼	cup olive oil
1	clove garlic
¼	cup diced onions
2	tablespoons diced green peppers
¼	cup diced celery
½	cup crushed tomatoes
1	bay leaf
	Salt and pepper
¼	cup sherry wine
6	(7-ounce) sole fillets
2	tablespoons diced prosciutto
2	tablespoons grated Parmesan cheese
1	cup breadcrumbs
2	tablespoons butter

Heat the oil in a skillet over medium-high heat. Brown the garlic and discard the garlic. Sauté the onions, peppers, and celery for 5 minutes. Add the tomatoes, bay leaf, salt and pepper to taste, and wine and simmer for 30 minutes. Preheat the oven to 375°F. Place the sauce in a casserole with the sole fillets on top. Mix the prosciutto, cheese, and breadcrumbs together and sprinkle on top of the fish. Add the butter and bake for 20 minutes.

MAKES 6 SERVINGS

Calamari Ripieni

(BAKED STUFFED SQUID)

Carbone's is famous for its fried calamari, without which no meal at the restaurant should begin. The kitchen also makes baked stuffed calamari that is a deeply satisfying main course.

3	*pounds squid*
¼	*plus ¼ cup olive oil*
1	*clove garlic, minced*
½	*cup chopped onions*
1	*basil leaf, chopped*
6	*anchovy fillets, chopped*
1	*cup breadcrumbs*
¼	*teaspoon salt*
¼	*teaspoon pepper*
2	*tablespoons chopped parsley*
½	*cup sherry wine*
½	*cup stock (fish or beef)*

The squid should be thoroughly cleaned. Have your fish market prepare it for you. Chop the tentacles and sauté in ¼ cup oil with the garlic and onions for 3 minutes over medium-high heat. Mix the basil, anchovies, breadcrumbs, salt and pepper, and parsley and add to the tentacles. Stuff the bodies of the squid with the mixture. Use toothpicks to hold the stuffing inside the squid. Preheat the oven to 375°F. Place the squid in a baking pan. Add the remaining ¼ cup oil, wine, and stock. Cover and bake for 30 minutes.

MAKES 6 SERVINGS

Gamberetto al Mario

(Pan Fried Shrimp)

A very simple and rewarding thing to do if you get your hands on some firm, fresh shrimp. The wine, oil, butter, and garlic exist only to halo the shrimps' naturally good ocean flavor.

32	shrimp
½	cup all-purpose flour for dredging
¼	teaspoon salt
¼	teaspoon pepper
¼	cup olive oil
1	clove garlic
2	tablespoons Marsala wine
2	tablespoons butter
2	tablespoons stock or water

Shell and devein the shrimp. Dredge the shrimp in the flour seasoned with salt and pepper. Heat the oil in a skillet over medium heat, brown the garlic, and then discard the garlic. Sauté the shrimp until cooked, about 8 minutes. Add the wine, butter, and stock. Simmer and stir gently for 2 minutes.

MAKES 4 SERVINGS

Frutti di Mare Posillipo

(SEAFOOD POSILLIPO)

A delicious stew for clam lovers. We serve it with lengths of crusty bread suitable for dunking, mopping, and shoveling stuff from the bowl.

¼	cup diced celery
¼	cup diced carrot
1	clove garlic, minced
¼	cup diced onion
1	tablespoon virgin olive oil
1	tablespoon butter
6	extra large shrimp
4	sea scallops
6	littleneck clams
10	mussels
4	ounces large-cut calamari
¼	cup diced fresh fennel
½	cup dry white wine
	Pinch of red pepper flakes
¼	cup chopped fresh basil
1	cup pomodoro or marinara sauce

Sauté the celery, carrot, garlic, and onion in the oil and butter over medium heat until tender. Add the shrimp and scallops. Cook for 2 minutes and add the clams, mussels, and calamari. Cook 3 minutes more. Add the fennel, wine, pepper flakes, basil, and sauce and simmer for 10 minutes longer. Serve over pasta or as a stew with bread.

MAKES 2 SERVINGS

Pesce Spada con Verdure e Gamberetti

(Swordfish with Vegetables and Shrimp)

Swordfish lends itself to preparations that are plain as steak and fancy as this stuffed version, which incorporates seasoned shrimp and cheese.

¼	cup white wine
½	cup oil
2	cloves garlic
¼	cup lemon juice
	Pinch of fresh rosemary
½	teaspoon black pepper
4	(8-ounce) pieces swordfish, thinly sliced

STUFFING:

3	to 4 large shrimp, chopped
¼	cup chopped onion
1	teaspoon chopped garlic
¼	cup chopped celery
1	medium tomato, chopped
¼	cup (½ stick) butter
	Zest of 1 lemon
2	cups seasoned breadcrumbs
¼	cup grated fontina cheese
	Anchovy and Caper Sauce (see page 68)

In a bowl mix the wine, oil, garlic, lemon juice, rosemary, and black pepper. Marinate the fish for 24 hours.

To make the stuffing, sauté the shrimp, onion, garlic, celery, and tomato in butter over medium heat. Add the zest of lemon and mix in the breadcrumbs and grated cheese. Place the stuffing on the fish slices and roll. Hold together with toothpicks. Broil the fish for 3 minutes and finish in a 400°F-oven for 6 minutes. Prepare the Anchovy and Caper Sauce and pour it over the fish.

MAKES 4 SERVINGS

Gamberetto Rocco

(SHRIMP ROCCO)

Shrimp, garlic, and cheese melded in a pan of olive oil and butter. This favorite of Uncle Roc is an uncomplicated dish, but for those who want to focus on shrimp, it's a joy. You can serve it as an entrée with a side dish, atop pasta, or accompanied by tiles of garlic bread or bruschetta.

1	cup all-purpose flour
12	to 14 extra large shrimp
¼	cup virgin olive oil
½	tablespoon minced garlic
¼	cup sherry wine
1	cup grated Italian sharp cheese (Asiago)
¼	cup softened butter

Flour the shrimp and sauté in the olive oil over medium heat until three-fourths cooked. Add the garlic and stir 1 minute. Add the wine and cook 1 minute more. Add the cheese and butter last; stir well, and serve. May be served over pasta or with bruschetta.

MAKES 2 SERVINGS

Pesce Spada Incrostata di Pecorino
(PECORINO ENCRUSTED SWORDFISH)

The cheese gets good and crusty around the swordfish, adding a sharp, dairy-rich note to the meaty fish. The crust also serves to shore in the juices, keeping it moist.

1	cup all-purpose flour
4	(8-ounce) pieces fresh swordfish
4	eggs
	Salt and pepper
1	teaspoon freshly chopped sage
12	ounces freshly grated Pecorino cheese
⅓	cup virgin olive oil

SAUCE:

½	cup dry white wine
	Juice from ½ lemon
6	tablespoons butter

Preheat the oven to 400°F. Flour the swordfish. Mix together the eggs, salt and pepper to taste, and sage. Dip the fish in the egg mixture and then press into the grated cheese. Sauté the fish in a nonstick pan with the olive oil over medium-high heat (don't overheat the oil) until the fish is golden on both sides. Place the fish in a baking dish and finish in the oven for 6 to 10 minutes.

To make the sauce, drain the excess fat from the sauté pan. Add the wine and reduce by one-third. Add the lemon juice and butter. Stir until blended and serve over the fish.

MAKES 4 SERVINGS

Pesce Spada alla Genovese

(SWORDFISH GENOVESE STYLE)

Pesto became popular on Italian-American tables only in the last quarter-century, but it has been a staple of Genoa for a hundred years. The term "Genovese" applied to any dish usually means that it comes with a pesto sauce.

4	*(8-ounce) pieces swordfish*
½	*cup fresh basil leaves (about 12)*
1	*bunch parsley*
4	*cloves garlic*
½	*cup grated Romano cheese*
½	*teaspoon salt*
¼	*teaspoon pepper*
1	*cup olive oil*
¼	*cup butter*
¼	*cup walnuts, pine nuts, or almonds*
½	*cup sherry wine*
1	*small Spanish onion, sliced ¼-inch thick*
2	*tomatoes, sliced ¼-inch thick*
	Virgin olive oil

Preheat the oven to 400°F. Place the swordfish in a baking dish. To make the pesto sauce place the basil, parsley, garlic, cheese, salt, pepper, oil, butter, and nuts in a blender and process until a smooth paste forms. Top the fish with the pesto sauce and the sherry. Place the onion and tomato slices on top of the fish. Bake for 12 to 15 minutes. Drizzle with some virgin olive oil and the pan drippings and serve.

MAKES 4 SERVINGS

Merluzzo al Giardino

(COD "GARDEN" STYLE)

The "garden" here refers to carrots, zucchini, squash, and tomato that dress up the otherwise fairly bland cod. These are all vegetables that are common in backyard gardens in city neighborhoods as well as in the country.

4	(8-ounce) pieces cod
1	cup seasoned breadcrumbs
¼	cup (½ stick) butter
½	cup white wine
¼	cup fresh lemon juice
1	small carrot, julienned
1	medium zucchini, julienned
1	medium yellow squash, julienned
1	medium tomato, diced
¼	cup virgin olive oil
	Salt and pepper
	Lemon wedges for serving

Preheat the oven to 400°F. Place the cod in a baking dish. Top each piece of fish with ¼ cup of the breadcrumbs. Dot each piece with one tablespoon of the butter. Pour the wine and lemon juice in the pan and bake for 12 to 14 minutes. To prepare the vegetables, sauté them in the olive oil over medium heat until tender. Season with salt and pepper to taste. When the fish is done, place one-fourth of the vegetable mixture under each piece of fish, pour any pan drippings over the fish, and serve with lemon wedges.

MAKES 4 SERVINGS

Filetti di Pesce al Forno

(BAKED FILLET OF FISH)

This is a variation of the fillet of sole recipe on page 170, but with sherry wine added for flavor and aroma.

2	tablespoons olive oil
½	cup chopped onion
¼	cup chopped green pepper
¼	cup chopped celery
½	tablespoon flour
1	(28-ounce) can tomatoes
	Salt and pepper
1	bay leaf
1	whole clove
2	ounces sherry wine
3	pounds blue fish fillets
½	cup breadcrumbs
4	ounces ground prosciutto

Heat the olive oil in a skillet over medium heat. Add the onion, green pepper, and celery and cook until tender. Add the flour and cook 5 minutes longer. Add the tomatoes, salt and pepper to taste, bay leaf, clove, and wine; cook until thickened, 30 to 40 minutes. Preheat the oven to 350°F. Remove the bay leaf and clove. Put the sauce in a baking dish, top with the fish, and sprinkle with breadcrumbs and prosciutto. Bake for 30 minutes.

MAKES 6 SERVINGS

Tonno alla Griglia

(GRILLED TUNA)

While canned tuna has long been part of the Italian cook's repertoire, tuna steaks are a relative newcomer on Italian restaurant menus in America. Marinade gives these steaks a flavorful aura that blossoms on a hot grill.

½	cup virgin olive oil
¼	cup lemon juice
¼	teaspoon black pepper
½	teaspoon kosher salt
1	teaspoon chopped fresh mint
¼	cup soy sauce
	Pinch of red pepper seeds
2	shallots, minced
1	teaspoon minced garlic
4	(8-ounce) center-cut tuna steaks
	Lemon wedges for serving

Mix the olive oil, lemon juice, black pepper, kosher salt, mint, soy sauce, red pepper seeds, shallots, and garlic together in a mixing bowl. Place the tuna in the marinade for 3 hours. Grill the steaks to medium-rare and serve with the lemon wedges.

MAKES 4 SERVINGS

Filetti di Halibut al Forno

(BAKED HALIBUT)

A deeply flavorful casserole that combines the snowy meat of halibut with salty prosciutto, tomatoes, and peppers, making it thoroughly Italian in character.

2	tablespoons olive oil
½	cup chopped onions
¼	cup chopped green peppers
½	cup chopped celery
1	tablespoon all-purpose flour
1	(28-ounce) can diced tomatoes
	Salt and pepper
1	bay leaf
1	clove
¼	cup sherry wine
4	(8-ounce) halibut fillets
½	cup breadcrumbs
4	ounces prosciutto, chopped

Heat the oil in a skillet over medium heat. Add the onions, green peppers, and celery and cook until tender, about 3 minutes. Add the flour and cook 5 minutes longer. Add the tomatoes, salt and pepper to taste, bay leaf, clove, and wine. Cook until thickened, 30 to 40 minutes. Preheat the oven to 350°F. Remove the bay leaf and clove. Place the sauce in a casserole, top with the fish, sprinkle with the breadcrumbs and prosciutto, and bake for 30 minutes.

MAKES 4 SERVINGS

Gamberetti Piccante

(SPICED SHRIMP)

Love 'em or hate 'em, anchovies are impossible to ignore when they are part of any dish. Here, otherwise simply-cooked shrimp are given a shot of flavor by the inclusion of anchovies and capers. Serve this on a plate with risotto or another favorite starch, or use it to top a favorite pasta.

36	shrimp
1	cup all-purpose flour
2	tablespoons olive oil
2	tablespoons butter
4	cloves garlic
4	anchovy fillets
½	cup sherry wine
	Juice of ½ lemon
1	tablespoon capers
2	tablespoons fish stock
	Pepper

Dust the shrimp with flour. Heat the oil and butter in a skillet over medium heat. Brown the garlic and discard the garlic. Sauté the shrimp and anchovies in the hot oil over medium heat for 5 to 6 minutes. Add the wine, lemon juice, capers, fish stock, and pepper to taste. Sauté for 1 minute longer and remove from the pan. Serve immediately.

MAKES 4 SERVINGS

Sogliola alla Fiorentina

(FILLET OF SOLE FLORENTINE STYLE)

A la Florentine" is a term originated by French chefs to describe dishes served in the style of Florence, Italy—i.e., on a bed of spinach with a creamy or cheese-infused sauce.

8	*ounces ricotta cheese*
½	*teaspoon black pepper*
2	*tablespoons chopped Italian parsley*
2	*tablespoons grated Romano cheese*
2	*(12-ounce) packages fresh spinach, sautéed in olive oil and drained*
6	*(7-ounce) sole fillets*
1	*tablespoon chopped fresh basil*
½	*cup sherry wine*
¼	*cup seasoned breadcrumbs*
2	*medium tomatoes, sliced*

Preheat the oven to 475°F. Mix together the ricotta cheese, black pepper, Italian parsley, and Romano cheese. Place the cooked and drained spinach in a casserole. Spread the ricotta cheese mixture on top. Place the sole on this mixture and then sprinkle with the basil, sherry wine, and breadcrumbs and top with the sliced tomato. Bake for 15 minutes.

MAKES 6 SERVINGS

Salmone Piccante con Carciofini

(SPICY SALMON WITH ARTICHOKES)

Italian cooks make good use of artichokes, not only as a dish unto themselves but as a flavor and texture addition to other things. This salmon piccante gets a lot of its flavor from the grilled artichoke hearts plus, of course, the prosciutto.

¼	cup virgin olive oil
1	cup all-purpose flour
4	(7- to 8-ounce) salmon fillets
2	ounces julienned prosciutto
½	cup white wine
8	grilled artichoke hearts
¼	cup lemon juice
2	tablespoons capers
½	cup (1 stick) butter
1	teaspoon chopped fresh parsley

Preheat the oven to 400°F. Heat the oil in a skillet over medium heat. Flour the fillets and sauté them in the skillet with the prosciutto for 3 minutes on each side. Place in a baking dish and bake for 4 to 6 minutes. In the skillet that the fish were sautéed in, add the wine and reduce by half. Add the artichokes, lemon juice, capers, butter, and parsley and stir well. Pour over the fish and serve.

MAKES 4 SERVINGS

Salmone en Paste Phyllo

(SALMON IN PHYLLO)

Once strictly a signature of the Greek kitchen, see-through-thin phyllo dough has become a favorite "wrap" for chefs practicing cuisines of the world. Carbone's uses it to enclose salmon fillets packaged with artichoke pesto, zucchini, and squash. Each baked package is a virtual meal unto itself.

ARTICHOKE PESTO:

8	artichoke hearts
½	cup grated Romano cheese
⅓	cup virgin olive oil
¼	cup fresh lemon juice
½	teaspoon chopped garlic
1	teaspoon chopped fresh dill
4	(7-ounce) salmon fillets
1	zucchini, sliced lengthwise ⅛-inch thick

1	yellow squash, sliced lengthwise ⅛-inch thick
16	sheets phyllo dough
	Salt and pepper
2	eggs, beaten
4	lemon slices

Prepare a grill to hot, when your hand can only stand it at grill level for 2 seconds. Make the artichoke pesto. Place the artichoke hearts, Romano cheese, virgin olive oil, lemon juice, garlic, and dill in a blender. Process until smooth. Refrigerate until ready to use.

Grill the salmon to rare, about 2 minutes per side, and chill until cool. Grill the zucchini and squash until they are halfway cooked, about 3 minutes per side, then chill. Lay out phyllo in four stacks with four sheets for each stack. Preheat the oven to 400°F. Place a salmon fillet in the center of each phyllo stack. Spread a fourth of the artichoke pesto on each fillet. Layer zucchini and squash on each stack. Salt and pepper each portion to taste. Fold the phyllo over the fish and vegetable stack like a small package. Brush with the egg mixture. Bake for 8 to 12 minutes. Serve with the lemon slices.

MAKES 4 SERVINGS

COFFEE AT CARBONE'S

Coffee service is noteworthy among the many modern dining concepts instituted ahead of their time by Carbone's. Coffee at Carbone's is far more than just an after-dinner eye-opener—making and serving it is given a place of significance. Evening celebrants often request coffee served tableside with flaming brandy. The most spectacular example is Carbone's own "Italian Coffee," made with Galliano and Kahlua. Even patrons who do not conclude their meals with a "lightshow," enjoy carefully and expertly prepared coffee more typical of a coffeehouse barrista than of a full-service restaurant.

This has always been the case, long before Starbucks was everywhere. In 1988, on the restaurant's fortieth anniversary, Anthony Carbone described his restaurant's coffees as its showboats. "They are unique creations designed for our special customers," he wrote. "Cappuccino is named after the Cappuccino monks who liked dripped espresso sweetened with cocoa and topped with steamed milk." In addition he said, "The American version of espresso requires a lemon twist. A true Italian will put a lot of sugar in his coffee but not stir it, drinking it down only to the residue on the bottom."

· Desserts & Coffee ·

(Dolce e Caffe)

Crêpes
Strawberry Filling
Zabaglione
Angelo's Molten Chocolate Cake
Panettone Pudding
Tira Mi Ju "Pull Me Down"
Tiramisù "Pull Me Up"
Pumpkin Cake
Anise Cookies
Italian Cookies
Flaming Cocoa
Cappucino
Italian Coffee
Jessie's Coffee

Crêpe

(Crêpes)

Back in the days when tableside service was introduced, flaming crêpes were a house specialty. They remain an essential building block for all kinds of desserts.

½	cup all-purpose flour
½	teaspoon salt
2	eggs, beaten
1	tablespoon sugar
⅔	cup milk
1	tablespoon melted shortening
½	tablespoon grated orange rind

Sift the flour before measuring. Add the salt and sift again. Combine in a separate bowl the beaten eggs, sugar, milk, and shortening; add the flour to the mixture and beat thoroughly until smooth. Add the orange rind. Pour some of the batter into a hot, greased crêpe pan, tipping the pan to make the pancake as thin as possible. Cook until browned on both sides. Refrigerate until ready to serve. These are great filled with Strawberry Filling (see page 188).

MAKES 6 TO 8 CRÊPES

Ripieno di Fragola

(STRAWBERRY FILLING)

Billie Carbone, the original baker at the restaurant when it opened in the 1930s, used to make chiffon pies long into the night on busy weekends. This is her recipe for strawberry filling for crêpes.

1	tablespoon butter
2	tablespoons sugar
3	tablespoons anisette
2	tablespoons brandy
3	orange slices
4	crêpes (see page 187)
1	cup fresh strawberries, quartered
	Whipped cream

In a large frying pan melt the butter and add the sugar. Stir in the anisette and brandy and ignite. Crush the orange slices into the flame with a fork and discard the orange slices. Heat the crêpes in another pan. Place some strawberries in the center of each crêpe. Spoon the flaming sauce onto the strawberries and top with the whipped cream.

MAKES 6 TO 8 SERVINGS

Zabaglione

(ZABAGLIONE)

When we make zabaglione, we like to play with liquors," Vinnie says. "We use peach or pear liqueur, and always Marsala wine. We like it best served over fresh berries."

8	egg yolks
4	tablespoons fine sugar
1½	cups Marsala wine
⅓	cup Galliano liqueur

Beat the egg yolks and sugar and cook in a double boiler over medium heat until white. Stir in the Marsala and Galliano, whisking constantly until the mixture is thick and forms peaks. Serve over fresh fruit of your choice in a champagne glass while the Zabaglione is still warm.

MAKES 6 SERVINGS

Torta al Cioccolato Fusa di Angelo

(ANGELO'S MOLTEN CHOCOLATE CAKE)

These individual cakes, served warm with vanilla ice cream, are small symphonies of chocolate within chocolate: a chocoholic's delight. Angelo, for whom they're named, originally came to Carbone's as a plumber, which he was by trade. But once he had the opportunity to ply his skills as a pastry chef, he became a key player in the kitchen.

	Butter to grease cups plus 1 cup (2 sticks)
	Powdered cocoa
12	*ounces semi-sweet chocolate*
⅔	*cup sugar*
6	*tablespoons cake flour*
3	*eggs*
6	*egg yolks*
1	*teaspoon vanilla extract*
6	*Dove Promises candy or chocolate ganache*
	Vanilla ice cream

Generously butter six (4-ounce) custard cups and dust with powered cocoa. In a double boiler over medium heat melt the chocolate and remaining 2 sticks of butter. Remove from the heat and stir in the sugar. Preheat the oven to 375°F. Stir in the flour, eggs and egg yolks, and vanilla. Pour the batter into the cups and press a candy piece into each one. Bake for 15 minutes. Invert onto plates and serve warm with a scoop of vanilla ice cream.

MAKES 6 SERVINGS

Budino al Panettone

(PANETTONE PUDDING)

Panettone is a multipurpose sweet bread that is served as a snack with coffee, as dessert, or as part of a bread basket. It is usually made in a circular shape and dotted with pignoli and citron, and it is a fundamental part of celebration meals around Christmas. It also makes a terrific basis for bread pudding, as evidenced by this custard-rich Carbone's dessert.

1	*(2-pound) panettone, cut into cubes*
3	*extra large eggs*
8	*extra large egg yolks*
5	*cups half-and-half*
1½	*cups sugar*
1½	*teaspoons vanilla extract*
1½	*teaspoons ground cinnamon*
	Sweetened whipped cream or ice cream for serving

Preheat the oven 350°F. Place the panettone cubes in a 9 x 13-inch pan. Wisk all the remaining ingredients together and pour over the bread. Let the cubes soak for 10 minutes and then cover the pan with foil. Place that pan in a larger pan filled with 1 inch of hot water. Bake for 45 minutes. Uncover the pan and bake for an additional 45 minutes, or until the pudding puffs and the custard is set. Remove from the oven and cool slightly. Serve warm with sweetened whipped cream or ice cream.

MAKES 8 SERVINGS

Tira Mi Ju

("PULL ME DOWN")

Tiramisù—meaning "pull me up"—grew tremendously popular in Italian restaurants in the 1990s. As a variation on that dessert, Carbone's came up with Tira Mi Ju, which they say means "pull me down." It is a similar kind of pudding that is made richer and more dense by an infusion of that favorite Euro-spread, Nutella.

1	(8.75-ounce) container mascarpone cheese
3	egg yolks
3	tablespoons sugar
1	cup sweetened whipped cream
1	(7-ounce) package ladyfingers (Savoiardi)
3	cups sweetened hazelnut coffee (cold)
1	jar Nutella (warmed in a double boiler)
	Powered cocoa

Mix the mascarpone, egg yolks, and sugar in a bowl. Fold in the whipped cream. Dip each ladyfinger fully into the coffee and arrange a single layer in an 8-inch square dish. Drizzle half the warm Nutella over the ladyfingers and cover with half of the mascarpone mixture. Repeat with another layer of coffee-soaked ladyfingers. Drizzle on the remaining Nutella and top with the remaining mascarpone mixture. Refrigerate covered for at least 3 hours. Before serving, dust with cocoa.

MAKES 10 TO 12 SERVINGS

Tiramisù

("PULL ME UP")

Vaguely similar to British trifle, tiramisù is a fragile pudding made with coffee-soaked ladyfingers, creamy mascarpone cheese, and chocolate. Delicate in texture and light in weight, it is nonetheless a deeply satisfying way to end a meal.

---

1   *(8.75-ounce) container mascarpone cheese*

3   *egg yolks*

3   *tablespoons sugar*

3   *cups sweetened espresso coffee (cold)*

1   *cup sweetened whipped cream*

1   *(7-ounce) package ladyfingers (Savoiardi)*
     Powered cocoa

Mix the mascarpone, egg yolks, and sugar in a bowl. Fold in the whipped cream. Dip each ladyfinger fully into the coffee and arrange a single layer in an 8-inch square dish. Cover with half the mascarpone mixture. Repeat with another layer of coffee-soaked ladyfingers. Top with the remaining mascarpone mixture. Refrigerate, covered, for at least 3 hours. Before serving, dust with the cocoa.

MAKES 10 TO 12 SERVINGS

Torta di Zucca

(PUMPKIN CAKE)

This ethereal layered spice cake tastes especially fitting in the fall, and it is sheer delight accompanied by cups of powerful espresso.

CAKE:

2¼	cups all-purpose flour
2	teaspoons baking powder
2	teaspoons ground cinnamon
¼	teaspoon ground ginger
¼	teaspoon allspice
½	teaspoon salt
¾	cup pumpkin
⅓	cup sour cream
⅓	cup honey
1	teaspoon vanilla extract
¾	cup (1½ sticks) butter
1¼	cup sugar
3	eggs

MOUSSE:

2	plus 2 cups heavy cream
2	cups whole milk
½	cup sugar
8	ounces white chocolate, chopped
4	tablespoons gelatin
1	tablespoon vanilla extract

Preheat the oven to 350°F. In a large bowl, sift the flour, baking powder, cinnamon, ginger, allspice, and salt. In a separate bowl, mix the pumpkin, sour cream, honey, and vanilla. With a mixer, cream the butter and sugar until fluffy. Add the eggs and mix in the flour mixture alternating with the pumpkin mixture. Bake for 30 to 35 minutes or until done. Let it cool for 10 minutes.

While the cake is cooking, make the mousse. Simmer 2 cups heavy cream, milk, and sugar in a saucepan over medium heat. (Do not boil.) Stir in the chocolate. In a separate bowl combine 2 tablespoons of water with the gelatin. Let it sit for a couple of minutes, then microwave it for 20 seconds to melt. Add the gelatin to the cream mixture and let it cool in the refrigerator for 30 minutes. Whip the remaining 2 cups of heavy cream and fold it and the vanilla into the chilled gelatin mixture.

To assemble the cake, when it is cool slice it into three layers. Place one layer in a 10-inch springform pan and cover with the mousse. Repeat this step two more times. Chill for 8 hours.

MAKES 16 SERVINGS

Biscotti all' Anice

(Anise Cookie)

Biscotti means "twice baked," referring to the fact that these cookies are made in a loaf, then baked and sliced and re-baked until crisp.

5	eggs
1	cup sugar
¼	teaspoon anise oil
1	teaspoon baking powder
2	cups all-purpose flour

Preheat the oven to 400°F. Beat the eggs until thick and yellow. Add the sugar gradually. Add the anise oil. Sift the baking powder and flour together and add to the egg mixture. Flour a cookie sheet. This batter is to be poured onto the cookie sheet in 5-inch strips. Bake for 15 minutes.

MAKES ABOUT 30 BISCOTTI

Farfallette Dolci
(ITALIAN COOKIES)

Absolutely basic sugar cookies, made with plenty of butter and shortening, are what you want to nibble at the end of a long meal, after dessert, with second, third, and fourth cups of coffee. They also make a nice little snack any time of day.

6	eggs
3	tablespoons sugar
¼	teaspoon salt
½	teaspoon vanilla extract
3	cups all-purpose flour
2	tablespoons butter
3	cups hot shortening
½	cup confectioners' sugar

Beat the eggs lightly. Add the sugar, salt, and vanilla and blend thoroughly. Place the flour on a board. Cut the butter into the flour. Make a well and add the egg mixture. Knead until a smooth ball is obtained. If soft, add more flour gradually to make it firm but not hard. Set aside for 30 minutes and then cut into four sections. Roll on a well-floured board until wafer thin. Cut into 6-inch strips ⅜-inch in width. Tie into a bow-knot shape. Fry in the hot shortening until light golden. Drain on an absorbent paper towel and cool. Sprinkle with the powdered sugar.

MAKES ABOUT 40 COOKIES

Caffe Diablo
(FLAMING COCOA)

We won't say this recipe should be tried only by licensed pyrotechnicians, but we will say that flaming things is not a cooking process we recommend to the inexperienced chef. Many of the staff at Carbone's can tell you of the time that a waiter was asked by a large party to make its Caffe Diablo extra spectacular. He flamed it so well that the sprinkler system got tripped, dousing a room full of people with water.

1	lemon
1	orange
8	cloves
1	tablespoon sugar
1	cinnamon stick
3	tablespoons Galliano
4	tablespoons cognac
1	tablespoon Grand Marnier
2	cups black coffee

Peel the lemon and orange. Stick the cloves into the peels and add to a chafing pan with the sugar and cinnamon stick. Pour the liqueurs into the chafing pan and ignite, being careful not to burn the peels. Add the coffee and serve.

MAKES 4 SERVINGS

Caffe Cappuccino
(CAPPUCCINO)

There is an episode of the TV show *The Sopranos* in which Pauly Walnuts grows furious when he realizes that the Starbuck's chain has made a killing selling a product that he feels is and ought to be uniquely Italian: coffee drinks based on espresso. One of the most popular of these is cappuccino, made with steamed milk and a dash of chocolate—a favorite at Carbone's long before the rest of America learned to become Italian-style coffee hounds.

1	tablespoon sweet chocolate
6	tablespoons espresso
2	tablespoons steamed milk
	Ground nutmeg or cinnamon

Place the chocolate in a coffee cup. Add the espresso and steamed milk on top. Sprinkle with the nutmeg or cinnamon to taste.

MAKES 1 SERVING

Caffe Espresso
(ITALIAN COFFEE)

A glorious show in the Carbone's dining room, Italian coffee can actually be made without flaming the brandy. The fire does crystallize the sugar on the rim of the glass, which is a wonderful thing, but the intoxicating flavors of Galliano, Kahlúa, and coffee are delicious even if you don't risk a kitchen conflagration.

1	*lemon wheel to rim the glass*
	Sugar to rim the glass
1	*tablespoon brandy*
2	*tablespoons Galliano*
2	*tablespoons Kahlúa*
½	*cup espresso or dripped coffee*
	Whipped cream

Run the lemon wheel around the rim of a 7-ounce glass and then dip the glass in sugar. Place the lemon wheel on the rim of the glass. Pour the brandy into the glass and light it. Swirl the flaming brandy to crystallize the sugar and heat the glass. Pour the Galliano and Kahlúa into the heated glass. Add the espresso or dripped coffee to the liqueur and mix. Float the whipped cream on the coffee and serve.

MAKES 1 SERVING

Caffe Jessie
(JESSIE'S COFFEE)

Named for one of Carbone's longtime waiters who was known for his skill at making the after-dinner coffee flames lick up towards the ceiling, Jessie's Coffee is an intoxicating postprandial eye-opener that includes rum and Tia Maria as well as flaming brandy.

1	lemon wheel to rim the glass
	Sugar to rim the glass
1	tablespoon brandy
2	tablespoons Tia Maria
2	tablespoons Myers rum
½	cup black coffee
	Whipped cream

Run the lemon wheel around the rim of a 7-ounce glass and then dip the glass in sugar. Place the lemon wheel on the rim of the glass. Pour the brandy into the glass and light it. Swirl the flaming brandy to crystallize the sugar and heat the glass. Add the Tia Maria, rum, and coffee to the heated glass and mix. Float the whipped cream on the coffee.

MAKES 1 SERVING

Index